Climbing Adventures

CLIMBING ADVENTURES

A Climber's Passion

by JIM BRIDWELL
with Keith Peall

illustrations by John McMullen

ICS Books, Inc.
Merrillville, IN

CLIMBING ADVENTURES

Published by:
ICS Books, Inc.
One Tower Plaza
107 E. 89th Avenue
Merrillville, IN 46410
800–541–7323

Library of Congress Cataloging-in-Publication Data

Bridwell, Jim.
    Climbing adventures / by Jim Bridwell, with Keith Peall.
        p.   cm.
    ISBN 0-934802-22-X : $16.50
    1. Bridwell, Jim. 2. Mountaineers--United States--Biography.
I. Peall, Keith. II. Title.
GV199.92.B75A3 1992
796.5'22'092--dc20
[B]   92-17929
                                                                          CIP

DEDICATION

This book is dedicated to my wife Peggy. Many of the stories here were made possible by her support, patience and love.

Table of Contents

1 **Dance of the Woo Li Masters**
Desperation on the East Face of Moose's Tooth,
Alaska 1981 1

2 **Zenyatta Mondatta**
The first ascent of
an El Capitan testpiece 1981. 15

3 **Confessions of a Speed Freak**
Buzzing down California byways 1968 27

4 **Big Wall, Big Chill**
Bird returns to Half Dome 1987 37

5 **Tour de Force**
Aspen skiing, telluride ice and
shiprock sandstone 1974 49

6 **A Quiet Night in Buenos Aires**
Never give 'em money before
you get the goods 1978 69

7 **Cerro Torre—Alpine Style**
Going fast and light in
the Land of Tempest 1975 77

8 **East Face of the Fortress**
Epitaph of an expedition 1988 87

9 **Aquarian Wall**
An early first ascent in Yosemite 1970 93

10 **Shadows**
Hanging it out on Half Dome 1989 103

11 **Reservations**
To climb or not to climb
on forbidden rock 1977. 113

12 **Nose in a Day**
The first 24-hour ascent
of El Capitan 1975 125

13 **The Grand Master**
Reflections on the
Patagonia experience 1973 135

14 **Cerro Stanhardt**
Forging a new route
on one of the Torres 1988 151

15 **Desmochada**
Sun and storm drench a first
ascent in Patagonia 1988 161

16 **Strange Customs**
Many are the woes of
the international traveler 1980 173

17 **The Eiger, Climb for the World**
Jim and a senorita vie for leads on the fabled
North Face 1991 183

18 **Operation Edison**
Even the best-laid plans...1972. 197

19 **Largo's Apprenticeship**
A visit to Camp Four in the '70's 1970 203

About the Author 209

Jim Bridwell

One

The Dance of the Woo Li Masters Moose's Tooth—East Face

March 1981

A jet. Yes, I was sure it was a jet. The sound was only slightly different, but uniquely so, from the avalanches thundering down around us. I'd only recently seen huge tongues of boiling snow flicking out from the base. The airliner was probably heading for Oslo or some such place and would arrive in the morning or maybe in the evening. I couldn't figure out which, because that's the way jets are. You're never sure what time it is. My thoughts started to race into relations of time and its necessity for place but were harshly broken off as I realized I was looking down 3,000 feet to our tent. The spacious dome tent looked like heaven and we were in hell.

What was I doing in this "inhuman zone?" Was it choice, happenstance of fate, or a combination of these that brought me to meet Mugs Stump? Only four months ago we were strangers, first meeting in an outdoor cafe in Grindelwald, Switzerland. We drank strong coffee and shot the bull about similar experiences on the North Face of the Eiger. One cup of coffee equals about one hour of bullshit. Before three cups had been consumed, we were jawing about the East Face of the Moose's Tooth. Both of us had failed on this 5,000-foot face. At least we were in good company—we figured the face had been attempted over ten times by different parties, all very strong teams. We made plans, not for the Tooth, but maybe that's where fate or coincidence came to play its part.

In early March, Doug Geeting, owner of Talkeetna Air Taxi, flew us in his powerful Cessna 185 towards the great gorge. But when we located our planned objective it wasn't there; no ice had formed where we hoped to find it. Instead, all the faces were in the worst condition possible. A thin veneer of ice with a light dusting of spindrift powder clung everywhere; overhangs bulged with snow clinging incredibly to their undersides. It wasn't just bad, it was inhuman. What could we possibly do in these conditions? We had to think fast—Doug's a good guy but he wouldn't fly us around forever. The nearby Moose's Tooth beckoned. Its East Face appeared equally horrendous but we couldn't impose on Doug's patience any longer. It would have to do. These were the cards; we would have to play them.

Getting Geeting aloft after a smooth landing took some digging and pushing. As the plane sped away, we gazed in awe at the hoary specter before us. Just thinking about it made my bones brittle and my spirit fragile. My imagination balked at further inquest, and I set about erecting our beautiful North Star dome tent. At least our home on the glacier would be luxurious. The ogre above could wait for inspection until my courage was well braced.

The next day dawned clear and oh so cold. In March, Alaska still doesn't feel the sun; it passes but doesn't touch. I remember my hands freezing when I'd touched the metal of the Cessna the day before. They felt the same burn when I adjusted the focus ring on the spotting scope. There was no other phrase; it was fucking cold. The face looked impregnable and the invaders were armed with slingshots.

But we thought just maybe we could pull off the ol' David and Goliath sketch. We chose a route to the right of our previous attempts. Those technical aid routes were hideously plastered with ice and out of the question. Our new choice dictated a more perilous passage but it seemed the only plausible possibility. A lightweight alpine-style approach could be the key. We were bluffing with only a pair. Like grabbing a tiger by the tail, we couldn't let go or we'd be eaten. The lower half of the climb consisted of avalanche chutes and faces fed by the whole upper wall. If a storm came in while we were on the climb, retreat would be suicide. The only way down was up; conquest or death, so to speak. It sounded ridiculous but it was true. Retreat in good weather would be very difficult at best, but we wouldn't be retreating in good weather unless, of course, there was something up there we couldn't climb.

The barometer rose but the storms battered us without caring. We didn't mind. We used the time to psych up and sort out our gear. The minimum ruled: four days of food and fuel to be stretched to six or seven if needed. An austere allotment, food consisted of gorp and coffee with sugar, plus two packets of soup. The hardware rack was skeletal. We had trimmed away the fleshy bolt kit and second set of Friends, leaving the bones: ten ice screws, fifteen rock pitons, six wired nuts, one set of Friends and the essential Chouinard hook. We opted for a technical yet swift descent—hopefully not too swift—down a 1,500-foot rock face into the east couloir, rappelling mainly from slings draped over horns. This descent would also be suicidal in a storm as two huge faces on either side fed the couloir lethal doses of snow. But it did lead directly to the tent whereas the Bataan death march down the North Ridge led only to the homeless Ruth Amphitheater. We would choose when fate decreed.

Clear skies came but the first day we watched and timed the avalanches, attempting to glimpse the secret of the pulsating rhythms. That night we deliberated on whether to wait another day, as we consumed large quantities of whiskey. Something inside told me to go in the morning, perhaps the whiskey. It wields a strong opinion indeed.

We agreed and in the morning found ourselves trudging to the base, laboring under our packs and hangovers. I didn't want to know what I was doing until it was too late. Needless to say, Mugs did the leading while I did the motivating.

A 55-degree snow slope led to the steep, narrow ice venturi, 250 feet long, which collected every minute spindrift slough and amplified it into a blinding, freezing torrent of misery. Appalled and impressed, I watched

Mugs lead 75- to 85-degree ice without protection in waves of gushing spindrift with a 35-pound pack tugging at his shoulders. When it was my turn, I secretly hoped for a break in the avalanches, but I knew I would get my justice (my justice I have already chosen, as we all have). At first I thought I could wait out the rushing torrents. Soon I realized, like Mugs, that it was hopeless, but still climbed on. Frozen, I reached the belfry. My wooden fingers fiddled with the camera while simultaneously attempting to feed out rope.

After one pitch we climbed together to the first traverse. Steep powder covering sugar-snow over rock (sketchy to say the least) ended at imaginary belay anchors. Both leader and follower were, in fact, leading. With no protection, each was responsible for the other's life; mistakes weren't allowed. The first traverse, a long three pitches, led to a three-pitch calf-burner ice face and on to another horrid traverse that was worse than the first and even longer. Near its beginning we heard a shout. Our minds must be askew, yet it wasn't an alcoholic illusion. Some fellow mountaineers ski-touring up the Buckskin to the Ruth Amphitheater were shouting up to us. We yelled back and carried on.

Tenuous climbing crossed thin powder snow over hidden patches of ice and steep rock. Nearly non-existent protection interspersed similar belays. We had to have confidence in each other; retreat would have been nerve shattering. In places we climbed on two to five inches of snow over 60- to 65-degree rock. Often, to my distress, these pitches began with a downward traverse of 40 or 50 feet before going horizontal or upward. Near day's end we reached a steep snow slope where digging a bivvy platform was possible. Mugs fixed a pitch above for better anchors before we precariously nestled in. North Face, the climbing equipment and apparel manufacturer, had supplied me with a space-age sleeping system to test. A pleasant success, it kept me warm and toasty despite sub-zero temperatures, spindrift and all.

In the supremely frigid morning, we dared not move from our cocoons until the sun's rays renewed our hope for life. Frostbite was our imminent host if we dare break the house rules so we regulated our desires accordingly.

A steep, ice-choked chimney rose up out of our field of vision and tested our abilities for the rest of the next day. From below, I judged it to be about five pitches long, but it turned out to be seven rope lengths instead. This chimney, together with the headwall above, appeared to constitute the main difficulties of the climb.

I led the first and least steep section before the white ribbon bulged abruptly and obscured our inquisitive gaze. Mugs pressed the attack up the 80- to 85-degree slippery gouge. In places he encountered overhanging bulges which the cold, dry winter had metamorphosed into an airy, unconsolidated granola. A desperate struggle ensued at these overhangs. Ice axes and hammers became useless weapons against these fortifications. Forced onto tiny edges for crampon points and shaky pitons for hand holds, I often used my ice tool picks as cliff hangers on rock ledges or wedged in cracks, nut fashion. Especially useful for this technique, my Forrest Sabre hammer quickly gained favor on these pitches.

The assault continued into the failing light of evening. I became weak and nauseous from dehydration as our daily consumption of water was less than six cups per man per day. In those temperatures man's devices cease to function as they were designed. Now an ineffectual nuisance, the stove only boiled water after an hour of coaxing and shaking to warm it. We had penetrated into the inhuman zone and were paying the consequences.

Mugs had fixed the previous pitch and I'd swung around a corner onto a small 65-degree ice slope, the only possibility for a bivouac. A precarious perch took hours of ice sculpting in the dark. We slept late. At almost 1:00 p.m. we started the tedious struggle for liquids, then ascended the fixed rope to our high point. Vertical ice reached upward and once again Mugs valiantly met the challenge, leading two pitches up the icy serpent. The twisting, curving corridor exited onto an easy snow slope, which extended to a formidable headwall. Even with the telescope we hadn't been able to probe the secrets of this section of the climb. Intuition lured us right, up an ice runnel onto a snow rib. I poked my head around the corner only to be confronted by a steep rock wall. Its thin cracks were well armored with ice and presented a chilling specter of extreme difficulty.

I tensioned off a nut for which I'd chopped a spot in the rock. My thinly gloved fingers searched for usable rugosities while my crampon claws scratched at scaly granite. I laybacked a steep flake, only to find its top closed with ice. Desperately, I clung with one hand while I perforated the ice with a hammer, probing for a secure spot. Standing on an icy shelf, I caught my breath and scrutinized the wall now confronting me. Moving right to a groove, I aided and free climbed before swinging left to a small ice ledge. After putting in some anchors, I called Mugs up.

Only a portion of the next lead disclosed itself and it didn't look promising. Mugs moved off hooks onto the fragile thinness of precarious ice. After 40 feet of slow, begrudging difficulties, he shouted down that it was blank above. From a gray sky snow began to fall. Retracing our steps now spelled disaster. We needed a bivvy site and there was none below us for many pitches. A night spent exposed and standing in slings would devastate our bodies in their present weak and dehydrated condition. We had to push a passage up now—and quickly!

"Are you sure there is no possible way?" I queried.

"Let me take a good look, I gotta figure this out," he replied.

He moved only occasionally, but at least some progress was being made. What was he doing? I could only imagine the worst. He called down for a #3 Friend, so I climbed up, took out the belay anchor and sent it up. Hanging from slings off a tie-off draped over a nub of rock, I continued my frigid vigil.

Above me, the Friend popped into a shallow hole, then a hook move led to a shaky knife blade placement behind a half-inch flake. Several more technical aid moves later Mugs, after two hours of nerve-grinding climbing, reached an ice tongue that led to easier ground. I sped to the belay and started the next pitch as quickly as possible. Impending darkness meant we had to find a place to bivvy soon. The now-heavy snow fall caused spindrift avalanches to cascade over us with increasing regularity. Marginal climbing traversed across a slab covered with four inches of snow. I hoped for some ice below the snow but no such luck!

I splayed my feet duck-style to attain the most purchase. Amazingly, they stuck to the slate-roof-like surface thinly covered with snow. Once past this section I encountered a trough filled with bulletproof ice. By this time I was extremely sick. Mugs came up and found me slumped over, weak and nauseous from dehydration. He led the next two pitches of steep mixed ice and rock. My strength ebbing, I followed the last rope length by headlamp. Fortunately we had found a place to dig a snow cave—a gift from heaven.

After two hours the snow cave was completed. We brewed tea and coffee, two of the worst drinks possible for dehydration. At 1:30 a.m. we collapsed in our sleeping bags secure from the storm.

Life revived slowly the next morning. From my vantage point near the cave entrance, I could see the storm breaking up. Sunshine seeped through the thin, diffused clouds, but I kept the vision secret from Mugs: I wanted to rest a little longer. The sunlight crept into the cave, making it impossible to hide the beautiful weather. Crawling out at 11:30 a.m. we commenced climbing.

Route finding problems confronted us. Picking the easiest and not always most obvious way is a talent born of experience and oft times luck. Our luck held and by 3:30 p.m. we stood at a spectacular vantage point on the top of the Tooth. I took one photograph after another until two rolls of film and an hour had disappeared.

Suddenly Mugs coyly asked if I wanted to start down. The weather was clear in all directions; it was also fairly late and I was tired, but secretly I had a sense of foreboding about the descent. Feeling a possible ordeal lie ahead, I quickly said no! Stifling my suspicions, I explained that it would be a technical and potentially difficult descent and we should allow a full day because there would be no place to stop once we started. Mugs agreed, and we returned to our photography.

Darkness came sneaking over the mountains when our stove begrudgingly produced two cups of tea without sugar. Our supplies were nearly finished so getting down was imminently important. We burrowed deep into our survival cells as the cold became increasingly bitter. Temperatures plummeted to 30 degrees below zero during the night and the wind continued, waiting for some exposed skin in the morning. Truly tortuous packing got us ready to go the next day. All man-made gadgets ceased to work, another wonderful quality of the inhuman zone. The stove managed two cupfuls of cold water before it died.

After overcoming a snow slope we began rappelling over discontinuous snow and rock bands. As we descended rappel after rappel, the snow disappeared leaving the kind of rock for which Moose's Tooth is famous: crumbling and rotten. The face steepened and disappeared below us, making it impossible to see where we were going. I kept angling left because the couloir for which we were heading came up from the left. The rock had become devoid of cracks with a few scabs of very flexible, rotten flakes. Alarms went off in my head, activating my whole being into survival mode.

Rappelling past an overhang and tension traversing left to a flake-like ledge, I pounded two pitons into compressed gravel and wondered what to do next. Looking down I could see nothing to go for. I thought of the bolt kit stashed below. Mugs had wanted to bring one but I had insisted that it was unnecessary and too heavy. This was Alpine Style—you know, watch the weight, count every match and all that jive. My mind raced in all directions at once like a trapped cat in a corner—the word "frantic" might best describe my reactions.

Computer-like I made a decision and yelled up instructions to Mugs. I asked him to tie one rope off to his anchors and to send the other rope down the single nine-millimeter rope. I'd rappel down 150 more feet to see what I could see. If I saw nothing I would jumar 300 feet back up to Mugs. We would then have to climb ten pitches or more to the summit and look for another way down. This devastating course of action would require the rest of the day and part of the next.

Once on the newly fixed rope, I tensioned left again and then climbed up and left, my crampons screeching and snarling on the rotten granite as I searched for tiny holds. Placing a #3 stopper in the only available spot, I clipped the rope through and continued rappelling. Near the end of the rope, a small but solitary flake came into view. I stopped and stared at it, hanging on the rope while a sad, sweet rhapsody of feelings and emotions washed over me. Catatonically, I remained there motionless with visions of people I knew and loved and to whom I owed love. It's sad we don't appreciate the trivial, yet wonderful and beautiful duties of life, like saying "hello" or washing dishes. We do them without paying attention. Thoughts rustled through my mind. My intuition had been correct. We had come to meet our ordeal.

I glanced up and saw clouds preying on the sky. Then I started up the rope but stopped automatically, turning to take one last look at the flake. Reaching the nut I had placed, I unclipped, swung back right, continued up to the two piton anchors, and yelled for Mugs to come down. I actually woke him up—he had fallen asleep from the excitement. He could hear the uncertainty in my voice. When he reached me, I explained the situation before we pulled the ropes through; I wanted him to partake in the decision. Once we pulled the rope there would be no choice. He had an easy way of boosting my confidence while accepting my course of action, whatever I might choose.

Casino time—one roll of the dice for all the marbles. I said a prayer to myself before starting down. Retracing my traverse, I reached the single stopper I'd previously fixed and brought Mugs down to a minimal stance. He surveyed the anchor briefly with wonder, tempered by doubt. I shrugged my shoulders and said, "That's it." My heart tried to escape from my mouth for the next 150 feet until I secured a #1 Friend behind a small flake I'd seen from above. I placed another nut while Mugs duplicated the rappel. He later told me that he'd almost unclipped from the anchor but quickly realized that a fast death was more appealing than a slow, agonizing but inevitable one. After descending half the rope, I gave thanks to the merciful one for wonder of wonders, the ropes reached a snow-covered ramp. The chilling grip of death relaxed. A calm peace soothed my quaking soul. Now a routine descent, within two hours we were galloping through deep snow towards the security of our tent.

Everything in the tent was frozen. We immediately fired up the stove and began guzzling brew after brew of hot liquids. We laughed and joked until late into the night. Our five days of intense experiences required time to unwind. The cards were played; we drew aces. Finally, I collapsed into prone paralysis. Just before unconsciousness, the memorable words of French climber Jean Afanassieff came to mind, "This is the fucking life, no?"

Two

Zenyatta Mondatta

1981

The summer in Tahoe had been the hottest I could remember, a radical departure from Alaska in March. Since becoming a jet-set climber, I'd become used to such contrasts, so that my body was constantly adapting to the variety of climactic conditions.

Because of these traumatic oscillations (as well as laziness) I decided to take the month of July off. This gave me the opportunity to relax with my family and, at the same time, casually organize equipment for a new route on El Capitan. In January, Peter Mayfield, Craig Calonica and myself had climbed the first six pitches only to be stormed off. We had covered only half a pitch of new ground as another team had pioneered the first five and a half pitches the previous winter. I was anxious to get back but the three of us hadn't been able to get together. Meanwhile the Park Service was becoming understandably annoyed with our gear, which was still hanging down the face and beginning to elicit inquiries from the tourists. Due to scheduling conflicts, I replaced Craig with Charlie Row, another climber with the necessary experience. Although I hadn't climbed with him before, I knew from his reputation that he had the right stuff and was easy to get along with. This was important as the remainder of the route would take many days to complete.

August found me driving my old Dodge station wagon along Highway 395 toward Yosemite. I stopped briefly at Tuolumne to collect Peter, but stayed long enough to drink quantities of alcohol with Ron Kauk, which enabled him to demolish his nearly new truck later that evening.

Peter drove down to the Valley as I had difficulty seeing past the dust on the windshield. The next few days we peacefully occupied ourselves making copperheads, cabling rurps, and collecting and packing the last few items of gear before going up the fixed ropes. Weighed down and pouring sweat, we dumped our bags at the base and looked woefully at the bottom end of our fixed ropes swinging forlornly 20 feet above our heads. Some clever assholes had pulled the end down and stretched the line as far as they could before cutting it off. Presumably this was done to keep us from going up our ropes as the 15 feet or so of rope would hardly be worth the effort, even to the poorest of beggars. They didn't know how difficult it is to outfox an old fox. We attached a Petzel ascender to the end of a section of pipe, locking the cam open. We then released it onto the end, using a piece of dental floss to activate the trigger. Within a few minutes the end of our rope was rescued from the zephyrs. With biceps bulging with lactic acid, I reached the top of the three ropes which had been tied together to reach the ground. They hung 50 feet out from the wall at the base; the knots were passed while hanging in space. This was no place for those with a faint heart.

We spent the night comfortably in our Cliff Dwellings, produced and sold by Mike Graham and a vast improvement over the old hammocks. At sun-up Peter and Charlie ascended the last fixed rope while I packed the haul bags. The first lead had been granted to Charlie, since all the pitches looked extreme it didn't matter who led. After he started tapping it out, I came up to wrestle with the bags.

Steep, continuously thin pitoning led directly toward the long, white roof above. A short blank stretch had to be strenuously negotiated using the drill. The drilling was not without merit though, as the bolts provided the first real security in 70 feet. Charlie's body was already wracked by cramps when 45 feet of gymnastic antics, on paper-thin flakes, were required to finish the unrelenting pitch to the small stance at the right end of the roof. Charlie's lead of the first new pitch on the route impressed me as I cleaned the pitons and I told him so. By the time I arrived at the belay, it was getting late, so I slapped in a pin to haul on (and to beef up the belay), while Charlie readied the rappel to the bottom of the pitch. I always sleep better with the knowledge that two sets of anchors are supporting my little separate reality.

Once the dwellings were set up, food was passed around, accompanied by conversation about the day's events. It had been slow going but I was pleased, both with our progress and with the minimum number of holes drilled so far. A pitch per day may seem ludicrous to the uninitiated, but first ascents of this extreme nature require at least twice as much energy, concentration and usually time than do subsequent ascents.

Breakfast next day was an early affair. By the time the sun found us Peter had started the next lead. An almost invisible hairline crack led straight up the porcelain-colored overhanging wall to a giant flake that was detached on either side. Paying careful attention, he worked slowly upward on rurps and special tiny copperheads tailor-made for this particular circumstance. The pencil line he followed ran up 40 feet to where it had been erased, forcing Peter to move to the right on hooks. Everything fit together beautifully. A couple of dowels and a few more hooks enabled him to reach the great double-edged flake. Though the climbing became easier, surmounting the flake was a long, awkward process.

After the anchors were placed I jumared up a free hanging rope to scope out the next lead while Charlie de-pegged Peter's pitch. The features I would be nailing appeared very thin indeed and it was reasonably late in the day. Although I wanted to jump on the sharp end of the rope I decided to leave it until the next day, as there would probably be nothing substantial to retreat from if it got dark halfway through the lead. There was no real hurry yet. We had taken food and water for seven days and could easily stretch it to eight if need be, so we stopped early, setting up the bivvy for a leisurely night.

In the morning I prepared myself. Nothing was said but I knew that everyone had to be aware of our situation. Each rope length overhung the last, making retreat impossible. We were committed. Our situation inspired and required us to continue upward. Above, the flake Peter had been following arched left and disappeared. I was forced directly up a thin corner using rurps, knifeblades, and copperheads. From where this corner ran out, I saw another dangling flake, 25 feet above me. Good fortune had it that this blank section was not entirely without weaknesses. A disconnected series of subtle slopes allowed passage across an otherwise featureless wall, using hooks and only one drilled hole. Fascinated and exhilarated I pieced the puzzle together and watched the pattern of the route unfold. The continuity of the pitch endured, yielding our third consecutive A5 lead. Anchored to three bolts, I viewed the rock above while Charlie jumared up. My vista gave no intimation that things would change, but this was in fact the beauty of the route. One never had something for the mind to cling to with hope. Here and now was all there was. The top and bottom, the beginning and the end.

When Charlie arrived, he started surveying the wall above while I perfunctorily organized the paraphernalia onto his hardware slings. From my top anchor Charlie placed a machine bolt rivet in a shallow drilled hole, the protection we used in all the drilled holes apart from belay stations. Carefully placing the spring-loaded cams of a Friend behind a horridly thin fin of rock, he inched his way up. I had confidence in Charlie's abilities now, and quickly snapped a few shots of Peter cleaning my pitch as Charlie worked out his next placement.

Suddenly, the hideously familiar sound of someone falling—the chaotic rattle of hardware—filled the air. I automatically ducked into the rock to brace for the impact of a 170-pound mass but, to my surprise, nothing happened Instead, off to my right a body sprang into view, bouncing abruptly at the end of a nylon cord. I had forgotten about two fellow climbers doing the Zodiac, 150 feet away. This, their first big route, would likely linger in their memories for some time to come. I asked if everything was all right and he assured me that all was well.

Charlie's concentration was so complete that he took no notice of the brief drama. Two hours of toil and sweat brought him to the doubtful security of a blank section of rock, which occurred at the halfway mark on the rope. He agreed to place a rivet and lower down to me. As another day neared its end, we all needed a well-deserved rest. Each in his turn slid down the cord, turning like spiders in space. The destination was not only below, but 60 feet to the right of our self-made plumb line. While hanging on the rope, an arc had to be calculated in order to arrive exactly at the bivouac. Otherwise, after pulling 60 feet sideways we would find ourselves embarrassingly above or below the desired position.

By dusk, we were all safely attached and pleasantly prone in our dwellings, swapping food and experiences. The night sucked us quickly into a coma.

Golden rays beckoned our stiff bodies into action. Another day of nerve-tingling adventure awaited. Sometimes I feel that climbing is not so much a matter of courage as a function of adrenaline addiction. Whatever the truth of that, Charlie soon got his morning fix. The air was still, hot, and quiet except for the occasional tune of the hammer tap-tapping. Within two or three hours my legs were quite stiff. I was thankful to be able to move when Charlie established the next belay station. Peter jumared up, and prepared to lead while I cleaned the pitch. After many comical gyrations and a few scary moments, I too reached the belay just as Peter started climbing. Noticing that the anchors, except for one bolt, were all straight down behind one huge expanding flake, I decided to haul and hang the bags on a couple of different hooks. From the look on Charlie's face I noted that these unusual tactics met with his approval.

Peter's boyish face and stature are merely a disguise for the tiger that lurks inside. A blank stretch of rock only makes him hungrier for some really desperate aid to sink his teeth into. He soon found his meat in the form of copperheads, tied-off knifeblade tips and blind hook moves on a steadily overhanging wall.

After a knifeblade traverse under a long, thin ceiling, he disappeared onto a slab to set the belay for the fifth A5 pitch in succession. Everyone was giving 110% of themselves, as was evident in the standard of climbing being produced. Subsequent ascent teams are well advised to do several other of the more difficult aid routes on El Capitan or Half Dome before attempting this one. An hour later, after several broken drills and many swear words, Peter had three bolts in the steel-like skin of the slab.

Although late in the day, the corner above drew me irresistibly onward like a moth to the flame. Despite some difficult climbing in the first part of this corner I made good progress and was soon about 90 feet up. Peter and Charlie tied another rope to the end of the lead rope and lowered me gently through the air to their waiting grasp. Fully stretched, our arms just touched, enabling them to pull me into the slab. I like overhanging routes—they allow one the luxury of a mistake whereas otherwise long falls might be fatal.

Sleeping against a slab such as this would normally be a miserable plight, but fortunately, the Cliff Dwelling was designed with adjustable hanging straps which compensated for almost any angle of wall. We had a comfortable night's sleep, waking refreshed, with a good chance of finishing the climb that day. I completed my previous day's lead within an hour. Charlie quickly came up to start the next. The angle of the wall lessened above and although the top was still out of view, I could feel its presence. Climbing steadily at first, Charlie soon slowed to a snail's pace as the route became difficult, circuitous and constantly demanding carefully calculated choices. Slowly, stubbornly, the rock submitted to Charlie's persistence. After several hours, another rope length was finished, giving us our first sight of the summit since leaving the Valley floor, nearly a week before.

Suddenly I could feel my emotions struggling with the tentacles of desire. Summit fever had weakened my control and the beast of anxiety ran untethered within my mind, free to slaughter the calm. Nearly as fast as it had started, the battle inside ceased when the route deadended, forcing Peter down. We would not reach the summit that day. The human animal whimpered back to its primordial cave, relinquishing command again to the slightly battered mind master.

The next morning Peter chose the less obvious way, and soon arrived at the summit. Due to terrible communication, I waited until the haul bags moved before beginning to clean the pitch. Poor Charlie had to rescue the gear from the incorrect route of the day before, a task I could tell he loathed to do. As soon as I reached Peter, we shook hands, Stonemaster fashion before ferrying gear to a safe place away from the edge. I stopped when I heard Charlie screaming from below. Carefully, since I was untied, I leaned over the edge and deciphered his desperate cry for a belay from above. A promptly lowered rope effected the rescue. Soon Charlie's perturbed face popped over the top. We all congratulated each other on the great route we had done and busily began sorting and repacking the gear for the ritual air drop.

Two Frenchmen, who had arrived in the meantime, watched with curiosity, overtaken by amazement, as we heaved our two haul bags over the side. We had attached a parachute, fashioned from rain flys, to each bag to slow their descent. Carrying light loads, we started down with the two young Frenchmen. They hadn't made the descent before so we offered to show them the easiest way down. When we reached the car all of us felt too tired to hike up the talus to fetch the haul bags so we planned to retrieve them in the morning.

The five of us jumped into the car and headed for the store to buy the necessary beer for a traditional celebration. Massive quantities of alcohol were consumed, but not, of course, in excess.

I wish the story ended here on a happy note, but this was not to be. Upon our arrival at the base of the wall we were amazed and disgusted that one of the haul bags containing $2700 and 27 years worth of hardware had been stolen. After several days of accumulating facts, we concluded that three climbers (I use the term with reservation), who had been fixing pitches on the Tangerine Trip, were responsible. But the evidence was circumstantial, therefore nearly impossible to pursue further. It is saddening to admit that Yosemite is no longer a place where climbers can climb with feelings of trust and brotherhood. I left Yosemite with $20 in my pocket, three bald tires and little desire to ever return. Paradise Lost.

Three

Confessions of a Speed Freak
1968

High beam lights probe the unyielding night. The massive eight-cylinder engine feeds the power of herds of wild horses to the fat, squat tires that propel 6,000 pounds of uncompromising Detroit steel along the endless highway....

It seemed endless to me that summer, anyway, as I commuted grimly between the Southern Desert and the High Sierra along the all-too-familiar Highway 395. I found plenty of time for reflection during these lengthy solo trips (ten hours at legal speeds, though I usually did better). I reflected, among other things, about the attitude of many of my younger climbing friends toward the mechanized behemoth I drive. Gas guzzler? Well sure, but built to last, and still going strong after two decades. How much energy and resources are wasted in building vehicles destined for the scrap heap after five or ten years? These and similar thoughts coursed through my mind as I sped through the long night, fighting back sleep as I focused doggedly on that hypnotic white line unfolding implacably before me.

I like to think that I am more or less immune to nostalgia, a vice of those who are afraid to face the future or deal with the present. Nonetheless I couldn't suppress an errant, heretical desire for a simpler time, a time before the energy crisis, a time when ecology was just a word. A time of ignorance perhaps, but a time of innocent pleasure. There was only one imperative then: Go fast.

Before succumbing to the subtle lure of the rockface, my ambition had been to become a race car driver. Long before I discovered the painstaking, patient skills of climbing, where success and satisfaction are acquired slowly and grudgingly, I was captivated by the overt glamour and instant gratification of speed. I thrived on the thrill of maneuvering a car quickly and safely through the twists and turns of California's byways. Even after discovering the exacting delights of vertical navigation, the journey to and from the climbing area was an important part of the experience.

Naturally there were some unfortunate incidents during the learning process. On one occasion, I had the use of my father's Pontiac Tempest while he and my mother were on vacation. My use of the car was on the strict understanding that I wouldn't drive it outside our home town. A few hours after my parents' departure I was heading for Yosemite with a light heart and a heavy right foot. As I surged up the long incline at Pacheco, with Chuck Berry's distorted tones pounding from the single speaker, the automatic transmission shifted obediently down to second. I fidgeted in my seat, impatient with the long, tedious, uphill grind, looking forward to the fast downhill stretch to come. Over the top I flew, foot glued to the floor.

"Maybelene, why can't ya be true?" boomed out of the overworked speaker. Yaaa—hoo! This is the fun part! Sweeping wide turns, flat-out speed, loud music. Bliss! But what's that? Something distracting glimpsed out of the corner of my eye. I turned to look. A car keeping perilous pace with me, the driver gesticulating frantically, mouthing desperate words. As I punched the radio off in order to hear him I got the message. Without the music's blare I could hear a horrendous, grinding, clanking sound from the engine. Oh shit! I should have eased off the gas at the summit to let the transmission shift up again. The engine must have been screaming its little heart out, drowned by the raucous sounds of rock 'n roll. I pulled over and killed the motor. Well, not really,—the motor was already dead judging by the thick black smoke that billowed from beneath the hood. My first thought was less of paternal retribution than of a weekend's climbing ruined. Can't let that happen.

Resignedly, I hiked to the nearest telephone where I called a buddy back home who I cajoled into picking up the car and towing it back to town. Undaunted, I proceeded to hitchhike the rest of the way to the Valley.

I was lucky to have such an understanding friend to help me out. Dad was less understanding, although once the initial storm died down I came out with my hide more or less intact. The same friend owned a Tiger, basically a Sunbeam Alpine, a British wanna-be sports car which had been given some real teeth by being fitted with a 289-cubic-inch Ford engine. This gave it a power-to-weight ratio which was more than adequate for dangerous driving. We liked to drive up to the Guadaloupe Dam and see how fast we could make it. As this tortuous trail had plenty of blind corners, we drove it at night so we could see by the headlights if anyone was coming the other way. We only needed half the road, but preferred to take our half out of whichever side suited us.

I enjoyed driving the Tiger, but was usually restricted to Dad's '68 Tempest. One night I borrowed it to take a spin into a rural area close to home. I was doing fairly well, at least for a while, slamming into bends and powering out of them, but I just pressed the old Pontiac too hard on one tricky turn. This was between the hillside and the bordering orchards that stretched for miles over the surrounding lowlands. The road sign said 10 mph, but I came confidently in at 40 and lost it. The vehicle slued broadside into the orchard on my left, narrowly missing the apricot trees ranged in formal ranks at right angles to the highway. I sat helpless as I felt the tires dig into the rough ground. I thought for sure that we were going to roll, but somehow we lost sufficient momentum and the car jolted to a halt. Both tires on my side ripped from the rims as I sat canted over at a crazy angle, my fingers locked to the wheel in nervous reflex.

That was the end of the fun for that night. I tried to open the door but the angle of the car was such that the bottom stuck into the newly plowed earth. I clambered across the seat and escaped through the passenger door. The exhilaration I had felt while driving ebbed quickly as

I stood in the chill night air and fished in the trunk for the spare wheel. As I dropped it on the ground I could tell something was wrong. Even on this soft, yielding soil there should surely have been more of a bounce to it. I kicked the tire, experimentally at first, then vengefully as the truth became clear—as flat as yesterday's beer. Cursing, I scrabbled around in the dark trunk finally unearthing the jack. A few moments work had the car raised high enough to remove the rims. Far fewer moments elapsed before the jack willfully toppled over in the soft earth, lowering the car gently to the ground. Cool as the night was, I felt sweat break out as I struggled to remove the jack from under the chassis. No go, it was pinned fast.

A cigarette soothed my tattered nerves. Fortified, I set off to check out my surroundings. Eventually I stumbled (literally) across the remains of a fence. Brute force, coupled with a latent talent for vandalism, soon furnished the materials for a lever.

"Give me a large enough lever and I could move the world," said one of the ancients. This character was doubtless in the first flush of enthusiasm for what would have been the newest of new-fangled technology. Then again, he may have been a salesman. I was inclined to the second theory as I struggled to lever the car from its dusty niche in Mother Earth, an earth that, despite its complete lack of moisture, seemed as tenacious as quicksand. If that oldster had been able to watch my desperate efforts, he'd have had to think up a new slogan. More likely, he would have got out of the lever business altogether. I wished I could but had no choice in the matter. Sweating blood, covered from head to foot in the fine apricot-grove dust, I worked on, mocked by the sweet scent of crushed fruit underfoot. Finally I managed to raise the stubborn weight of the chassis as far as I needed.

With a tire on each shoulder and a rim in each hand, I trudged to the nearest service station. Fortunately that phrase still had some meaning in those days. Not only did I get the wheels fixed, but after giving a dramatic account of my plight, I got a ride back to the car and a hand with remounting the wheels. Even so, it was late at night when I eventually slipped into the house and into bed.

"You should be more careful how you park that car," my dad grumbled the next day. "You've scuffed the whitewalls against the curb."

On occasion I managed to catch some of my friends in a weak or desperate moment and persuade one or more of them to ride shotgun on the way to Yosemite. So it was that I picked up the Bircheff brothers early one Friday evening. Phil, who had lost the ritual fight for the front seat, climbed bravely in beside me and double-checked his seatbelt. His brother Dave huddled in the back seat frantically pulling sleeping bags and foam sleeping pads over himself.

The journey passed virtually without incident for a couple of hours, but I wasn't quite up to my self-imposed timetable. I fretted behind the wheel, impatiently waiting to slide past one slow-poke tourist after another on the winding road between Briceburg and Cedar Lodge. Finally I saw my chance. I floored the gas pedal to pull out alongside the column of crawling cars. Impatience had clouded my judgement though, for a hulking semi-truck hurled around the approaching curve long before I reached the head of the line. None of the tourists had the wit to make room. I hesitated a nano-second before wrenching the wheel violently to the left. We slued across the path of the klaxon-blaring monster, skidding to a halt in a dense cloud of dust on the soft shoulder on the wrong side of the road.

"Nice moves, Bridwell," Phil observed dryly as Dave whimpered in the rear. Gravel spurted from the wheels as I pulled back onto the highway.

"Quit bitchin'," I replied. "We're still alive. No harm, no foul."

Not surprisingly, I wasn't alone in my passion for cars and speed; this was America, after all. Many of my fellow climbers shared my fascination and gradually an informal but hard-fought contest developed among some of us. The race was from Midpines Summit to the stone wall at El Portal, around 27 miles of hard driving. In some ways it wasn't a fair contest as we each drove very different vehicles with widely disparate characteristics and there was no handicapping. As I say, it was a loose, casual arrangement. The idea was simply to make the trip in the fastest time possible. Whenever one of us went to the Valley we logged our time on that stretch of road and relayed the results to our peers when we next saw them. We operated on the honor system—these were more innocent times.

I usually made a respectable showing, first in Dad's Pontiac, then later in my '56 Ford. Galen Rowell, who owned an auto repair shop, naturally had an edge when it came to tricking out his car with go-fast gadgets. Sheer speed, though, was less of an advantage than might be thought. The route was so full of twists and turns that cornering ability was more in demand, linked closely with steel-nerved skill, although good acceleration was useful. In the end, what mattered was not so much the car but the driver, his determination, flair and slightly crazed courage. The best times were often turned in by Frank Sacherer. He drove an old VW beetle, which he would fling into a turn so fast that the weighted rear end began to slide. Using a delicate touch on wheel and throttle he'd keep the ungainly vehicle just on the point of spinning out.

I was in Camp Four one weekend when he arrived with the news that he'd covered the 27 miles in just 27 minutes, at that time a record. Sacherer was pretty casual and laconic about it. His passengers, slack jawed and dazed, were simply speechless. I guessed they would be making alternate travel arrangements in the future. It took the accident of an inheritance to topple Frank from his hard-won throne. Danny Tavistock used his windfall to buy an AC Bristol Cobra which combined ferocious speed and acceleration with superb traction. As Danny proudly said, "This thing sticks to the road like shit to a blanket." Not even Sacherer's dauntless skill could prevail against the Cobra.

Frank's determined attack on the Midpines/El Portal speed record was quite typical of the man. By nature intense and driven, he approached everything he undertook with the same unrelenting seriousness. Eying me as I wolfed down a bowl of cereal outside my tent late one afternoon, he asked what I had climbed that day.

"Oh, nothing," I replied between mouthfuls. "Rest day."

He looked at me sternly, I believe he may have wagged a forefinger at me. "If you don't climb you shouldn't eat," he admonished grimly, before striding off for some boulder practice.

Four

Big Wall, Big Chill
1987

The sun was just starting to strike the wall, lighting up and revealing its secrets. I peered intently through the telescope, the reflector type that compels one to reverse the image for a true idea of what is being viewed. I then transferred the corrected result to a topo map that I drew on paper. It was painstaking work, but essential if we were to do the best possible job on this first ascent of a big wall route. It is often impossible to see which way to go when on the wall as bulges and roofs obscure the view. It might look very improbable when you are actually there, so a map is an important preparation for first ascents. I turned to my fellow climber.

"Want to have a look?"

Sean Plunkett slid eagerly into position. I began describing the intricate changes he was looking at, from nebulous feature to incipient crack. "Yes!" he exclaimed with each new revelation, but slowly and subtly I realized that we were on different routes. I had lost the lad 1,000 feet below.

"O.K., let's start again at the big roof."

This was Sean's first experience of a first ascent, of putting a route together in his imagination, creating it from the raw. His accomplishments were noteworthy yet I wondered how he would meet this new challenge. I couldn't know, not here on the ground. I always do the best job I can when establishing a new route, but for the finished product to have a uniform integrity, everyone who leads must also do their best. This, the first ascent, would be the only one in which we would be testing ourselves against the pristine stone, an artistic creation.

Climbers of the future will mime and either respect the original or deface it, rather like painting mustaches on the Mona Lisa. It takes experience and a coolness under fire to pull off a great route as opposed to a mediocre one. Sean was an aggressive, gung-ho type of guy who seemed to have a future in this game although I knew little about him. An over-zealous hammer could destroy more than it created. I would soon know what kind of aid climber Sean was since he would lead the next pitch. I had already fixed two pitches with Steve Bosque, one of the other members of the climbing team. Steve was a very good, experienced big wall climber as was Peter Mayfield, the fourth member of our Half Dome Expedition.

I had looked up at what would be the third pitch and could see that it was going to be difficult, most likely

P.D.H., meaning Pretty Darn Hard, part of a new rating system that we had decided was more applicable to modern aid climbs. The difficulty of a route changes, sometimes dramatically, from one ascent to the next, especially from the first ascent. So a number rating looses value and meaning, requiring climbers to fall and then take an average of distances fallen to accurately assess difficulty. The new system would give a basic feel of what sort of obstacles could be expected. The system contained only three levels: P.D.H., the most difficult; N.T.B., Not Too Bad; and finally N.B.D., which, of course means No Big Deal.

We carried more loads to the base, then spent a pleasant night under the stars, looking up at the bulk of Half Dome. In the morning, Peter and Steve returned to the valley floor for another load, while Sean began the next lead. Sean approached the wall like a college graduate going for his first job interview. He and his volunteer belayer, John Ottisson, ascended the fixed ropes while I positioned myself to take photographs. Shortly, they reached the high point and Sean started work. Moving slowly, he drilled some shallow holes to place the standard 5/16-inch machine bolts, the usual method for drilling on big walls other than for belay anchors. This is faster and maintains the continuity of difficulty on modern routes. He placed three of these before moving onto hooks, which have also become normal fare to the big-wall artist. He drilled again after three hooks and began vigorously testing the security of the placement. Suddenly it blew out. He should have flown for 50 but the hook held. Miracles never cease. The next time the bolt stayed in and he moved closer to the inverted staircase of disconnected roofs looming above him. These would be tricky. More hook moves brought Sean to a series of long reaches. Surprisingly, he passed the blank rock in between the roofs, doing a great job of leading. Only the final, largest ceiling remained to be solved. Swinging from knifeblade to rurp to copperhead he spun in the air with abandon, and emerged above the seeming impasse. He gave a rebel yell of triumph which I returned enthusiastically.

"P.D.H.... Yeah!"

When John had finished cleaning the pitch, they rappelled back to the ground. Sean glowed with pride; he had met the enemy and prevailed. I knew now that we had a real team, a team that would create a great route we would all be proud of.

We sat around the fire enjoying a feast and each others' company. The next day Steve fixed another pitch of P.D.H. It was slow going but I didn't care. Steve and I had been working for a concreting company for two years now and this was our vacation. We wanted to make the most of it. In any case, this type of climbing takes time, especially on the first ascent. The following day would mark our departure from the mundane routine of the commonplace, would see our lift-off into the realm of the fantastic.

The telescope had revealed the succulent fruit of blankness above, now it was mine for the picking. A single machine bolt off the station led to opulent hooking possibilities. Two rurps interrupted the series of 11 hooks, the last five of which were fine examples of artistic hook enhancement; 3/16-inch dimples on small knuckle-like bumps created a nearly invisible passage. The rope swung below me, unfettered by carabiners. I abbreviated the pitch by belaying below a huge roof, a fine place for the first bivouac since the ceiling looked circuitous, a waiting trap of dreaded rope drag. Since the last pitch had been a short 60 feet, I cajoled Steve into letting me lead the roof.

I started up and out the loose toothy blocks which hung in the roof. Care was essential here with Peter and Sean hauling the bags directly below, but the only tooth to fall was me. In the wink of an eye it was over, as was a 20-year record of no falls while aid climbing. All things must pass and so it was with the roof. I belayed 30 feet higher, from where I brought Steve up.

Steve led the next short pitch. He could have made it longer but experience told him to chose the natural belay instead of drilling anchor bolts higher up. We called it quits and went to help Peter's and Sean's epic battle with the haulbags. They had been confronted with the monumental task of hauling several hundred pounds of gear up to the first hanging bivouac. After surveying the problem, they felt it their duty to lighten the load by several beers each. With their judgment thus sharpened, they decided to divide the weight into two ponderous loads and winch it up double the normal distance. This process was still being refined when Steve and I rappelled down to help. Finally, after dark we collapsed into our hanging Portaledges exhausted and unorganized. The morning dawned clear, as is usual in Yosemite. We tried to find something to eat amongst the chaos in the haulbags. When Peter had eaten I reminded him that it was his turn to lead.

"Gosh, you're right, it is my turn," he said, then giggled, but the levity was short lived. Like a spider in space he disappeared over the roof. Sean followed and I saw neither of them for hours until I too emerged above the large canopy that obscured them. Peter, having already put in an honest day's work, was now on overtime. Slowly he made for the payoff. Thirty feet and an hour later it was over—the steepest pitch I had ever seen. What a way to not make a living. Sean started removing gear from Peter's pitch. As soon as he reached the steeply overhanging wall above the 5.10 slab, he encountered considerable problems reaching back in to retrieve the pitons. Peter rappelled down, like a plumbob marking true vertical, to take a few photos of Sean's gymnastic efforts. Once again we descended below the big roof for the night. Some order had been restored to the haulbags, allowing food to be accessed with efficiency. Sounds of snoring soon announced tranquility as I watched the automobile traffic in the Valley winding like a luminescent centipede through invisible obstacles.

We awoke to another brilliant day and passed around breakfast as we prepared for the work ahead. Sean and I went up to the high point, leaving Steve and Peter to pack and haul the bags. I don't usually climb in a foursome, but when I do I like the team to be spread between two sets of anchors. If we timed things right, Sean would be finished with the next anchors in place, before the others were ready to make the second haul. This procedure isn't essential but it is the best failsafe method and I sleep better for it.

Once again Sean tied onto the sharp end of the rope and started work while Steve and Peter hauled the bags from one belay to the next. We had adjusted to the routine and rhythm of big wall living. The mundane distractions of life in the flat world had been shed like a snakeskin. Sean struggled throughout the day, working hard to make each placement hold his weight, all 66 of them. I explained to him afterward that it would be better to make longer reaches and use fewer pitons. If none are likely to hold a fall, you merely increase the chances of falling by placing more. This makes sense in theory, but more seems better in practice. I knew the feeling and could sympathize, but nonetheless he had done two pitches worth of nailing and gained one in height. He finished the lead, putting a beautiful line of bolts up the next blank section, before rappelling down for our third night on the wall.

In the morning Steve and I ascended the ropes to start the next lead while Peter removed the gear from Sean's. The section above looked rather sketchy—maybe a lot of drilling. Thin at first, it went so well that I was able to move along quickly. We called this area the Pool Table for its flatness, but as I worked my way up features began to appear. I finished the pitch with time to spare and brought Sean up to continue. After 40 feet of difficult tapping, the light faded so we joined the others, two rappels below. The wall was always overhanging which meant that the ropes had to be anchored at the bottom to get us into the rock. Retreat was something we tried not to think about. Above, the route looked more promising and we banished such thoughts for the pleasures of stuffing our faces with food. It had been a good day, passing one of the doubtful sections on the climb with very little drilling. I felt confident that the one remaining questionable area, near the top, could also be resolved.

At daybreak Sean and I started packing the bags as the others made their way up the ropes. As Sean made the first haul, I leapfrogged above to begin the next pull. We had reached a narrow ledge the day before, the first thing we could stand on since leaving the ground. I felt spoiled, not standing in aid slings while I hoisted the sacks. Steve finished his lead before I had completed the haul, so I stopped what I was doing to lower Peter out and out and out—35 feet into space before he could ascend the rope up to Steve.

"Wow! I almost went for just stepping off the ledge!" he exclaimed.

"You'd look good with grey hair, Peter" I replied.

Peter hit some easy ground on the next pitch but still finished late. Sean started on the next lead in order to get a head start but was only able to complete half the pitch before waning light beckoned him down.

Catch Basin Ledge, as we named it, wasn't big enough to sleep on but it was scooped out, making it possible to dump and sort through the food. Since this was day five I wanted to inventory the supplies—hate crash diets. The next day progressed slowly, the small corner Peter was nailing closed up. Finally, he decided to try the Bird Beaks, the new pitons that I had fashioned from old Crack-'n-Ups. The Beak works like an ice ax or, more exactly, like a hook piton. As they were the only thing that worked, he used three in a row. It took most of the day for Peter to finish, leaving little time to start his attack on the next pitch. Afternoon clouds had begun to build, today they would dissipate, but my concern was that tomorrow it might rain on our parade. Under gloomy skies, Sean and Peter swooped down like Batman and Robin. Time had moved slowly for Peter today, he looked strained and tired, but happy. He could relax tomorrow during Sean's stint in the firing line.

There was a chill in the air when I awoke to a hazy July sky. Sean nervously started up the ropes. He knew what I knew; the next pitch would be difficult, perhaps as difficult as he could stand. It was all up to Sean. Leaving the belay, he began working his way up a series of very thin, loose flakes, like paper skins, they rattled and reverberated when the toes of his boots bumped them.

"I'm going to have to drill," Sean said, reaching for the bolt kit.

"What about over to the right?" I suggested.

He stopped reaching and looked right, then up.

"Maybe I can get something in here." Standing higher, he hammered the tip of a knifeblade in straight up. He hesitated.

"Go for greatness!," I yelled. "The opportunity doesn't come every day."

The wall was overhanging, he wouldn't hit a thing if he fell. He stood up. It held but it wasn't over. The pitch didn't let up, but neither did Sean. The most difficult lead so far, we called it The Paper Chase after the paper-thin flakes found on the pitch. Sean felt good about himself and the art he had created. Above, the mysteries of the most doubtful area of the route piqued my curiosity, but it would have to wait until the next morning. We were now occupied with getting the haulbags up in time to establish ourselves before dark. Working together, we just beat the black of night. I shared a communication with an unknown tourist below using my headlamp to flash a cryptic code which was answered in like fashion.

The next morning I climbed the first half of the pitch above. This quality pegging employed a full range of techniques and skills: long reaches, expanding cracks, and tension traverses using a wide variety of tools, including four of the new Beak pitons in a row. I turned a corner that blocked my view and my heart sank—blank! I expected a blank section but not like this. It was big, much bigger than it had appeared from below. The angle from which I had examined the dome had foreshortened the upper wall. I was worried, had I made other miscalculations yet to be discovered? Gauging the distance to the next nailable feature, I calculated the number of holes to drill. Thirteen times the drill bit into the onion-like skin of Half Dome and each hole left a scar on my ego. I did the dirty deed and descended, disgusted with what I had done.

Steve took the next lead while Peter belayed. We discussed which way the route should go above, although we could see our eventual destination 50 feet to our left. I explained exactly how the pitch should go. The team was doubtful but trusting. Hour after hour Steve worked out each placement. It would have been faster to have gone the other way but we weren't here for speed. What difference would a few hours make in years to come? It could only be done right this time. Late in the day Steve shouted down.

"You were right, this was the way to go."

Five

Tour De Force
1974

Halos glared, blurring the center lines in the road. My awareness pinballed between fear and bliss. The temptress sleep was all too familiar to me. So too was the terror of the consequences of succumbing while behind the wheel of a speeding car. Enduro driving was a necessary part of a lifestyle born of poverty. With no money to make ends meet, we relied on a razzle-dazzle mode of operation. A few dollars shy of a motel room, we drove through the night, me and Steve, trying to make it all work. Our target was an amigo's house a thousand miles away.

Steve McKinney was the world's fastest human on skis; seven times he had shattered the barrier. Mentally and physically, he had set the pace for the rest of the best. I was a rock climber, well known in Europe but here in the good ol' U.S.A... Well, here, more often than not, we were both defined as peripheral weirdo bums: Crazies. We could have moved to the Continent but I think we liked being "trapped" in a society that knew nothing of what we did and couldn't care less. We enjoyed a comfortable notoriety without paying the price of fame. It all made sense somehow.

I rolled down the window and stuck my head out, hoping the frigid wind would shock me awake. It worked for about ten minutes before I was again left to my own resources. I shook my head, slapped my face, sang along to the music that was already on the verge of blowing the speakers. I teetered before the abyss.

"Steve! Steve! Wake up!" I pleaded. "Ya gotta drive, I'm cooked." At four in the morning, I'd been at the wheel of La Bomba, Steve's 1970, 445-cubic-inch Buick Wildcat, for almost nine hours. The car was loaded with skis, boots, clothes, sleeping bags and climbing gear—all the accouterments for adventure except money. But we had friends, and we could get by with a little help...

Steve, still rubbing the sleep from his eyes, took the wheel while I crawled into the back seat among the mounds of gear and fell into the nest he had vacated. We hadn't far to go to our first stop—Chico's house in Aspen. Chico, an old ski racing buddy of Steve's, now made deer-skin Indian fashion statements for the beautiful people who flock to Aspen, a fashion statement in itself. At 5:50 a.m. we pulled up, bleary eyed, at Chico's place. I still hadn't slept, probably too wired up from my nine-hour stint at the wheel. Chico answered the door bare-assed naked.

"Hey man, come on in before I freeze my nards off." He grinned from ear to ear, giving us big hugs in the doorway. "What brings ya out this way?"

"I'm going down to Silverton to check out a speed track, and Bridwell's gonna take me ice climbing down by Marty's in Telluride," Steve replied as he strode into the kitchen. We knew Marty from Tahoe. An old friend of ours, she currently held the women's skiing speed record. We invaded the kitchen and pulled up chairs while Chico disappeared in search of a bathrobe.

"So, let's go skiing," Chico said when he returned, probably knowing we'd been driving nonstop and were highway basket cases.

Oh yeah, I thought.

"Sure," Steve said, mindless that I'd been driving all night.

Bastard, I thought, I'll be hanging on for dear life. Naturally, I wouldn't miss the fun. I asked Chico if he had any strong coffee and rummaged in my pocket for some more NoDoz which I'd been living on for the last six hours. While Chico put on the coffee we went to the car to fish out our boots and ski clothes. I bitched at Steve about having had no sleep, but he just smiled and said, "You don't have to go." Without waiting for a reply, he grabbed two pairs of downhills and strode to the door. "Testy bastard, he's just trying to see if I'll hurt myself," I muttered as I grabbed my gear and shuffled after him.

The coffee and NoDoz kicked in. We lingered over a stout breakfast for some hangtime, then set out for the slopes of Ajax mountain. A bracing chill in the air helped to clear my head as we progressed up the mountain via a series of chair lifts. On the summit at last, I slid from the chair and felt for the center of the skis. They were an old pair of Steve's, but new to me. I applied a soft edge to see how they turned. Like greased snakes; they were sweet. I looked up to see the rest of the crew swinging a big arc into a tree-lined corridor before disappearing from view. I pursued in a tuck position, trying to catch up. I swung the corner and they were gone, but I could tell which way by the impact they had left on the recreational public. I followed in their wake. The corridor opened out onto a broad, rolling slope and I could see them taking big air off the last roll before dropping into a twisting gully. Oh God! It was going to be a frightful day.

Rocketing over the final roll, I found myself flying over the heads of petrified tourists. With my legs pulled up to my chest, I exhibited near-perfect position. I extended, landing like a pro 60 feet down the hill. Pulling roller-coaster G's against the side of the gully, I compressed and accelerated to ungodly speed. Faster, faster—sometimes the thrill of speed overcomes the fear of death. I wasn't going fast enough because I was terrified. There was no time to think, only to react. I no longer looked for the others, I was hanging on for dear life, just as I'd foreseen. I tried to decelerate by swinging high speed turns against the sides of the gully. I careened from one side to the other, back and forth, back and forth. A road was coming up fast, too fast. If I made a check turn I'd be out of position. Hell, just go for it, and I did. E-x-t-e-n-d and suck it up. Holy shit! I sailed forever...

The slope I landed on was groomed, and wide, and crowded with skiers. I felt like a bullet in a forest of people. Shouts of outrage and squeaks of traumatized tourists echoed behind me. I could see the bottom now, so I started making sweeping arcs across the least congested sector of the slope. In the middle of a turn, while still doing a good 40 mph, I felt something amiss with my outside ski. Looking down, I saw with alarm that the heel binding had opened. The ski only remained on my boot because I was standing on it. One false move and a nasty eggbeater would surely follow, thanks to those old-fashioned safety straps. Gently, oh so gently, I shifted my weight, transferring most of it to my uphill ski, closing the radius of my turn in an attempt to slow myself. Miraculously, it worked. I pulled to a stop outside a restaurant at the base of the slope.

I stepped out of the skis, went inside and cowered at one of the tables, wishing I had the money for a shot of whiskey. Pumping adrenaline like a cat in a kennel, I could have used something to placate my frazzled nerves. I kept my eye on the door, expecting some outraged skier or ski patrolman to come in after me. I could have killed someone. I may have—for all I knew, some old person could be dying at that moment from a heart attack. Suddenly the door burst open, in fell Steve and Chico, laughing themselves silly. Steve doesn't exactly laugh in the familiar sense. It's more of a chuckle or a snicker but whatever you call it, it had him doubled over.

"That was great! You should have seen yourself! I wish I had a movie camera." Steve coughed out the words in staccato phrases, unable to speak properly.

"Where were you guys?" I demanded, more in curiosity than in anger.

"On the last road," Chico offered, ready to burst into giggles again. "Yeah, you should have a downhill suit if you're going to ski like that. You caught enough air off of that last road to be running in the Holmen Kollen."

"Very funny" I said. Steve, who could sense my growing annoyance, decided to gouge a little deeper. "Man you should have seen the people scatter. It was like watching a bowling ball."

"I was trying to catch air. Anyway, enough of that old news. Let's go back out before someone finds me hiding in here."

"Ya think we should go to a different lift, where no one knows what we look like?" Chico smirked.

"Well, I'd feel safer," I said.

"So would everyone else." Steve gibed.

We skied until 3 o'clock then split back to Chico's pad for a shower and a beer. I figured that afterwards I'd fall asleep but my internal clock had shifted gears, passing into another unfamiliar sleep cycle. Chico and Steve planned to go out on the town, a proposition rife with danger in a place like Aspen.

"No way," I said.

"Oh, come on."

"Well, maybe, just for a while."

Soon out of the door, we headed for trouble. Out until 2:30 a.m., we'd seen everybody they knew plus a couple of people I knew and we'd had more than a few beers too many. I hit the bed and was gone, in more of a coma than a sleep.

It felt as though I had only just closed my eyes. I opened them to find myself back behind the wheel of that big Buick. A nice car to drive, but better if I were fully conscious. Armed with a hot cup of java, I hit the gas pedal and the four big wheels rolled towards Telluride.

Hours and several cups of coffee later we wheeled through the streets of Telluride, once a mining town, now a trendy, touristy, destination ski resort. That Old West, down-home motif was the marketing strategy here, and it worked. Our first priority was to find a restaurant, all that coffee was eating at my stomach. We thought we'd try to tone down the pangs with a novelty—food. Prices weren't too touristy, so we decided to splurge. As our friends had been generous the previous night in Aspen, we hadn't yet tapped into our budget. We were rich, at least by our standards. Food felt foreign, though in a pleasant sort of way. Feeling fortified, we decided it was time to mosey along up to the canyon for a look at Bridalveil falls. In winter, the rush of water ceases, the torrent solidifies into a cascade of ice, providing a challenging, three-pitch climb. This challenge, together with the possibility of climbing Shiprock, a volcanic skeleton in New Mexico, were the reasons I had offered to come along as mainstay chauffeur on this whirlwind tour.

Sunday afternoon was quiet, even in this tourist-oriented hamlet. Most of the local people were up skiing rocks or still preparing for the slowly arriving tourists of a low snow season. We drove to the roadside behind town where a mining operation continues to pull ore from the surrounding mountains. The way was barred by a closed gate, so I parked the car in front of the "No Entry" sign. The mine was closed for the Sabbath, so nary a soul was about. We crawled under the gate and skied up the snow-covered road that led toward the hoary beard of ice clinging to the shady side of the canyon. Within half an hour we stood at the base of a very wet Bridalveil falls. Exceptionally, mid-afternoon temperatures were above freezing, even in the shade. Water showered down the route. We cached the climbing gear, planning to return in the frigid pre-dawn hours of the following morning. Rest was what we needed now and Marty's place would fill the bill. Luckily, for we were not expected, Marty and her husband were home when we arrived. I hadn't seen her since she'd left Tahoe, a few years earlier and this was my first meeting with her new husband. I at once found him comfortable to be around. Together, they had built the cozy log house in which we stood.

"You've been keeping yourselves busy." I observed,looking up at the large logs which formed the roof.

"We had help from some friends with those log beams," she confessed. "But besides the plumbing and electrical work, we did everything else ourselves."

" Great place," said Steve. "We're still living from hand to mouth in a Tahoe City trailer park."

"Hey, if you guys need a place to stay, you're welcome here," Marty's husband offered. Our surprise was feigned, though not our gratitude. We begged forgiveness for our unannounced arrival and chipped in some money for dinner. A brunette beauty with a Polynesian complexion and a wonderful personality, Marty was an excellent athlete as well as a lot of fun. If she'd had ice climbing gear, she would have joined us for the climb. Instead, she wanted to ski up with us the next day, just for the view.

After an early breakfast, we rumbled up the road through darkness in the big V8. People milled around the mine entrance, all bleary eyed as they waited for the coffee to kick in and clear the sleep from their eyes. An officious-looking man in overalls turned and came towards us as we skied past the open gate.

"Where do you think you're going?" he demanded brusquely, his voice betraying no hint of friendly intent.

"Up to climb the frozen water fall," I said, mustering my best cheerily innocent voice.

"Like hell you are." It didn't sound good. "Get your asses outta here. No trespassing. Don't you read? Or don't they teach you in California?" He'd seen the car's license plates, obviously he had an attitude.

"We have our gear up there," we pleaded.

"You can go see the damn sheriff but you ain't going up there."

The sheriff, when we found him, sounded like the guy's brother. Cut from the same cloth, I thought. But after treating us to an hour of lecturing, spiced with threats and dire warnings, he escorted us back to the gate. There, he instructed the supervisor to let us collect our gear and then get out.

Winding, narrow roads snaked through the mountains and once more the driving was a nighttime affair. The headlights probed through the inky darkness as I rotated the wheel through one turn after another. I preferred the demands of coping with the twists and turns of this back road to the hypnotic boredom engendered by a straight highway. I didn't ask why we hadn't stayed longer at Marty's, assuming that Steve was anxious to get to the speed track at Silverton. Neither of us had been there before, so what was entailed remained an enigma. Unknown radio stations flitted by as Steve twiddled the dial in a vain attempt to keep one tuned in. We were approaching the little town of Ouray when I noticed an unnatural thumping in the rear of the car, a flat tire no doubt. A cursory inspection confirmed this dismal fact. After changing the wheel by the diffused glow from the headlamps, we stopped in Ouray and curled up on the seats to sleep.

We awoke to find frost coating the interior of La Bomba. I turned the key in the ignition. After a grinding protest, the big engine sprang to life. Once at a gas station, we left the motor running so as to defrost the inside of the car while the tire was being fixed. The service station owner, a pinched-faced, little weasel of a man, tried to gouge us for a new tire when all it needed was a new valve stem. That and 50,000 miles less wear on the bald surface that now contacted the road.

"The nerve of that guy, trying to sell us a safe tire," I grumbled, as we ate breakfast in Silverton as a gesture toward spreading the wealth. Later, the local sheriff led us to the mining camp from where we could ski into the much-touted future speed track. The muddy dirt road ended at a locked, swinging gate, reminiscent of the one we had ventured past on our ill-fated Bridalveil exploit only the day before. This time though, we had approval. After donning our skis, we started gliding over the snow which, presumably, covered the continuation of the same dirt road. Nearly flat, the track led to a giant bowl, dominated in the centre by an impressive mountain, later to be renamed Velocity Peak. Even at first sight, it was obviously an ideal record-breaking speed track. In profile, its contours held the perfect ingredients: a large flat section at the base (an ideal run-out, deceleration area) beneath a steep slope that swept upwards nearly 3,000 feet to a couloir just below the summit. The high elevation meant thinner air, therefore less wind resistance at record speeds.

I followed Steve as he skied up. We had to make sure what we were seeing wasn't an optical illusion. As the slope steepened, we had to side step laboriously, taking 30 minutes to climb a quarter of the way to the couloir.

Steep, long and perfect—it was just as we'd thought. With our climbing skins still on our skis, we turned for a straight run down what we had climbed. In short order, we accelerated to forty m.p.h. at which time I pulled into a gradual uphill turn to avoid the potential disaster threatened by the sticky, wet snow at the base. Steve, on the other hand, had no such qualms. As he hit the wet snow, he performed the St. Vitus dance, his body jerking like a man being electrocuted. Aided by his amazing balance and incredible innate strength, Steve flew into the flats still standing. I had chosen the prudent turning point, but Steve was chattering with the enthusiasm of a demented chimp.

"We'll break the 200 km here for sure," he exclaimed, not giving a moment's thought to the near explosion he'd just escaped.

"Whadya mean, we?" I corrected.

"You should try it, " he coaxed. "After that stunt you pulled at Aspen this'll be easy."

A Dylan song came to mind. "One should never be where one does not belong," I quoted. Steve persistently tried to coax me but I ended the dialogue by saying, "I do enough dangerous things as it is and I don't need to spread myself any thinner." He laughed, assuming that I was making a joke. Soon, the afternoon shadows beckoned us to the car and on to our next adventure—Shiprock.

But first, we fulfilled our promise to the sheriff and informed him of our safe return from the reconnaissance. After that we set off for Farmington, the closest town to Shiprock. Darkness overtook us as the big car rolled out of the mountains onto the plains of the high desert near the New Mexico border. Farmington was hopping on Friday night. Young people and good ol' boys alike were cruzin' the main drag, sporting cowboy hats and driving pickup trucks. The flashing lights, neon signs and honking horns were unfamiliar sensory intrusions. We'd been in town no more than a couple of minutes when a truck full of teenagers pulled alongside.

"Oh boy, here we go—trouble." But I was wrong, sort of. They'd seen our California plates, and that to them meant wild dudes.

"You guys from California?"

"Yeah."

"Wanna-go-party?" Steve was about to say yes, thereby confirm their wildest expectations, but I intervened. I had noticed a movie theater on the next corner announcing Cheech and Chong on the marquee.

"Sorry," I blurted out, "we have to catch a movie, but thanks for asking."

I wanted to climb Shiprock and knew that potential disaster lurked in that pickup truck. A movie made more sense right now, was a logical excuse, and would kill a couple of hours before we drove out to the rock under the cloak of darkness. It's illegal to climb on Navaho land and Shiprock is the central power-point of the Navaho Indian religion, just as Mecca is for the Moslems, definitely taboo for us infidels. We needed the cloak of stealth to perform our act of sacrilege.

Meanwhile, the double feature gave us a vicarious view of what the teenage pickup truck might have led to, confirming that I had chosen the right course. After bolting down a burger at an all-night grease shop, we were on our way to the rock. It was night driving at its finest—a mission, a method and a wrong turn. We lost half an hour on the detour, but by 2:30 a.m., we were parked at our destination. Or nearly, we were near the south dike, one of the unique, primordial spines that finger out for miles into the flat desert from the castle-like volcanic plug that forms the superstructure of Shiprock.

Our plan? Simple: Jack up the car, remove a tire, block it with rocks, lock everything inside, then walk out and do the climb. The ploy was to try to look like innocent people with car trouble rather than climbers. Laden down by packs of gear, we picked our way in the desert darkness. Across the void, an alert mongrel barked a staccato warning of our subterfuge. The great monument appeared to be a mere stone's throw away. In reality, we spent more than three hours tripping through eight miles of sagebrush, arriving near the start of the route exhausted. Although I was tired, my sleep was fitful, I was disturbed by an oversight on my part. The climb required three ropes by formula: one to leave fixed at a rappel, to re-ascend later and two for normal rappel descent from the summit. We had only two.

I awoke without realizing I had even slept. I had blinked and the night was over. Steve groaned, rubbing his eyes.

"What time is it?"

"Seven, or just about," I mumbled. We hid the sleeping bags and packs, grabbed some equipment along with a rope each, then strode to the climb with mock assurance.

A stack of rocks denoted this old, classic route which had originally required several points of aid, now eliminated. Using the rocks as steps enabled me to reach some holds on the overhanging wall. I tied onto the rope and jumped to the first hand grips, pulled up again and made a dynamic lunge to the next set, three feet higher. Not pretty by modern standards but it worked, and I was too tired and groggy to give a rat's ass what it looked like. I stopped a short distance above, where I could help Steve over the steep bit with a couple of useful tugs. Our Tour de Force campaign across the West had taken its toll, he had no complaint about the added assistance from me. Steve's blatant honesty was impossible to hide; his face revealed his every thought, the impish smile he now wore said everything. Easy climbing led up a dark rock intrusion known as the black dike, which we followed for three rope lengths before traversing left and upwards. Soon we reached the rappel point, where we would have to leave one of our ropes. I had hoped that we should be able to re-climb this section without leaving a rope, but close analysis of this possibility as I rappelled down gave little hope. Grudgingly, we left the line fixed for our escape.

From here, an airy friction traverse led above a sobering 1,500 foot drop of yawning exposure. Though not extremely difficult climbing, the narrow ribbons of ice that had formed in places along the route added to our excitement. One thrilling section required that we step onto nubbins of rock that barely protruded out of the ice. From the small stance that marked the end of this pitch, I warned Steve to take care on the icy sections. His eyes got bigger a couple of times but his passage across was uneventful. To my left, a steep little step with an old expansion bolt revealed the way. The bolt had doubtless been used originally for direct aid. Now I had to think carefully in order to pass it without pulling on it.

"If you have much trouble there, just grab the bolt,"

I told Steve. Though a great athlete, climbing wasn't his forte and the step was both tricky and difficult. Taking my advice, he used the convenient bolt and soon surmounted the difficulty. Throughout the climb so far, we had found small patches of snow. Now, stepping out onto a sloping slab that should have been easy terrain, I was alarmed to find instead a dangerous ski slope. Our smooth-soled rock shoes were poorly suited for these conditions. One mistake by either of us would be fatal, as there would be little chance of stopping.

Before starting up, I warned Steve, unnecessarily I'm sure, not to slip. Any fixed anchors were now well hidden under five inches of snow so I moved carefully, kicking suitable steps for both of us to use in turn. Normally nonchalant, Steve followed with stress and concern written across his face.

Two rope lengths later we were once again on firm rock. It would be worse going down, I thought. Keeping this in mind focused my attention. Soon only one obstacle remained before the summit: An overhanging rock horn that had been aided on the first ascent with a few bolts. I decided that I might as well try to free climb it as I wouldn't be coming back to Shiprock in the foreseeable future. I left sling stirrups on the bolts for Steve as I worked out the gymnastic moves. More economic than static power, controlled dynos brought me quickly to the top. Using the slings, Steve grunted his way past the same strenuous section as speedily as I had.

We bagged it. From the top the starkly beautiful view of pool-table-flat desert stretched for 50 miles in all directions, broken only by the tentacle-like dikes of Shiprock itself as they radiated outwards for several miles before disappearing into the sea of sand.

The rattle of a two-stroke motor cycle shattered the silent void with uncouth irreverence, its origin hidden by the huge bulk of the rock on which we stood. My initial impulse was to hide, until I realized that if we couldn't see them, they couldn't see us. I wanted to spend more time on top of the world, remote and aloof, but the shadow of Shiprock was already creeping across the desert plate. We had to go.

With only the single rope, we'd have to use craft in order to get back down safely. The descent went smoothly at first, even the snow slope. Then came the crux: the rappels down to the traverse that would return us to the fixed rope. One rope doubled, being only half as long, would bring us short of our next anchor. My solution was to send Steve down first, on the full length of a single rope. I would then follow making two rappels on the doubled rope, placing an intermediary anchor near the end of the first rappel. It worked perfectly except that, Steve missed the location of the traverse, continuing past to another ledge on a long horizontal scoop 50 feet lower. I followed the same procedure as before, unaware of Steve's mistake. As I descended, I saw the place where he should have stopped. It wasn't obvious, I almost missed it myself. But there it was and where had Steve gone? I yelled down to ask if he was OK, and was relieved when I heard his answering voice. When I reached the end of the rope, there he was, huddled in a cave-like recess. Holding one end of the rope I dropped down to the ledge. Steve knew he had done something wrong but I said nothing—yet. A brief inspection told me that it would be difficult and dangerous to regain the traverse by climbing up. The alternative was to traverse the scoop. I left the rope hanging, telling Steve to stay put while I investigated, and edged right. Patches of snow guarded the passage, while 1,500 feet of air below my boot heels emphasized the danger. At the end of the scoop I peered around the corner. Hmm...maybe. A few iffy moves would get me to what appeared to be an easy gully that allowed access to the fixed rope. I retraced my steps to discuss the option with Steve.

Suddenly, without warning, my heart leapt into my throat as the smooth-soled shoes I wore slipped on a patch of snow. An involuntary gasp escaped my mouth as I thought I was away. Steve grabbed for me, his expression, as usual, betraying his emotions. Miraculously the skid stopped by itself. The incident was over before the adrenaline hit my heart. I was touched that Steve had been willing to sacrifice himself trying to save me. Foolish I thought, yet knowing that I would have done the same. I pulled down the rappel rope, having decided in favor of the scoop traverse. It was less difficult than I had at first judged and within 20 minutes, we were climbing the fixed escape rope. An hour and a half later we stood on the ground, gazing up.

Without a word between us we turned to retrieve our packs, ready for the hike to the car. Darkness fell like a sword as we walked over sagebrush-littered sand. From the summit of Shiprock I had looked at the trusty La Bomba, a tiny solitary dot parked on the thin line of straight road. Curiously, this sight had brought back memories of high school geometry class. The car was still poised atop the pile of rocks when we finally reached the great beast at 11:15 p.m. Fondly, I patted the hood as Steve jacked it up and replaced the tire. The engine roared to life before Steve had finished tightening the last lugnut. He threw his pack on the back seat and we sped away in a cloud of dust as distant unseen dogs barked in protest. La Bomba slid over the road with silky authority as I glanced in the rearview mirror, gloating at the hulking silhouette of Shiprock. I put my foot to the floor and heard rubber squeal. We had a thousand to put behind us.

Six

A Quiet Night in Buenos Aires
1978

The bar was awash. Harassed waitresses struggled through the noisy throng with drink-laden trays held skillfully aloft. Grim, set smiles were pasted onto tired faces as they dealt with the increasingly obstreperous crowd. Over the years Yosemite, once the almost private reserve of a handful of Californians, had begun to attract an ever-growing number of climbers from around the world. This evening, a blather of alien accents seethed in a confused murmur around me as I sat in the relative peace of a corner table. A southern drawl vied with a harsh yankee twang, slack jawed Frenchmen babbled. Nearby, a handful of addled Brits roared drunkenly, not quite drowning out the din from a table of demented Canadians.

"Like the bleedin' United Nations in here, innit mate?" came a cheerful, familiar English voice. "There'll be a fight before closing time, I shouldn't wonder," he continued, with what sounded like happy anticipation. The speaker squashed in beside me and shoved a half-full pitcher of beer in my general direction.

"Robbie! Good to see you." I grasped the calloused hand thrust towards me. Blue eyes twinkled from a guileless, open face framed by shoulder-length blond hair. Robbie could easily pass for a Californian, a surfer perhaps. That is, until he opened his mouth and the strangled vowels and swallowed word endings of his native cockney came tumbling out. We'd last met in Fitzroy Park a couple of winters past. He and his mates had enlivened many a drunken, hilarious interlude during the otherwise tedious spells of foul weather. It was always good to see Robbie again, doubly so now I thought. Maybe I could pick up some information about a trip I was planning for the coming season. But as usual, it was difficult to pin him down. He seemed reluctant to discuss climbing, preferring instead to make ribald remarks to and about the scurrying waitresses. Meanwhile, he chugged down glass after glass of beer from the frequently renewed pitcher. He muttered all the while about its inferior quality even as he sought to catch the eye of a passing waitress to signal for yet another refill.

"So anyway," I tried yet again." I'm going back down to the Fitz this winter."

"Wish I was," he mumbled, frowning at the empty pitcher.

"I thought you and the lads went down last year."

"Yeah, we didn't get much done though, bloody weather. Did you hear what happened to us in Buenos Aires?" He became more animated.

"No, but I guess I'm going to."

"Oh, you'll love this story, let's get a refill first though."

The beer duly arrived and I settled back expectantly.

"We were all pretty done in when we arrived, jet lag and hangovers. It's a long flight from the U.K., plus we had an alpine start in the morning to get the plane to Rio Gallegos, so we dumped our gear at the hotel and decided to grab a steak, maybe a couple of beers then get to bed early. Have a nice, quiet night for a change.

"Well, you know what they say about good intentions. By the third bottle of wine Mac and me were starting to perk up a bit. Mac wanted to go to this night club place he'd heard about. The other pair weren't too keen. Dave was nearly asleep as usual, Phil didn't look much better. I was still game though, there's plenty of time to sleep when you're dead. Who used to say that? Can't think of the name. He's dead now though. So, anyway, that was that. The B team sloped off to bed and left us to it.

"This night club was a bit of a low-rent job, but lively enough, noisy too. Mac liked that though, you know what he's like. That stereo system in his van cost more than the van did and he still blew out the speakers in a week. We had a couple of gold watches (Scotches to you) and the place took on a rosier glow. I still couldn't hear a word Mac said above the row, but that was no loss. I left him babbling to the barman—he must've been a lip reader—while I went to pay a quick visit. When I got back he was out on the dance floor with this little beauty, long black shiny hair, lovely little figure, gorgeous. When the music stopped I saw him bellow something in her ear and she slid off while he came over to me grinning like a fool. He grabbed my arm making 'let's go' motions with his head. We shouldered our way through the crowd to a table where Mac's dance partner sat with another little darlin'. Beats me how he does it, he's got a face like a bag of rocks and he's about as charming as a bucket of snakes, but he still manages to pull the birds.

"I don't know who ordered champagne but it soon arrived and plenty of it, local stuff but good enough; cheap enough too. The girls dragged us around the dance floor a few times and in between flirted and giggled and generally made us feel welcome. After a while, I began to realize that something wasn't quite right. They were just a bit too friendly if you know what I mean. Not really spontaneous, rather mechanical, slick, rehearsed, I suppose you might say... professional. I wondered whether Mac had caught on yet or if he'd known all along. Not that I cared much, the champagne was doing its stuff and I was ready for anything, even the slimy little shit that suddenly parked himself at our table. The girls sidled off to powder their whatsits. This creep told he was their 'manager'. Their time was valuable and so on, not exactly spelling it out in so many words, but if Mac hadn't got the picture before he definitely did now. We soon made a deal and the girls reappeared on cue and hustled us outside, I suppose their meters were running now. There just happened to be a taxi waiting out front and we all bundled into it.

"The driver looked about 12 years old but he was big enough to reach the gas pedal, judging by the way we took off. I began to wonder if he was at all familiar with the brake pedal. As drunk as I was I got more than a bit nervous, so it was a relief when we arrived at the hotel more or less intact. The driver discovered the brakes at last and celebrated by standing on them. We were both shaken and stirred when we climbed out, but we were gobsmacked when we heard the fare. He must have thought we were a pair of dumb tourists or so far gone in drink that he could take the piss with impunity.

"I could see this would take a while so I gave the girls my room keys and told them to start without us and we'd be along as soon as we'd straightened things out. Yes, I know—bad move. Not the silliest thing I've ever done, but fucking close. Mac and me can be fairly persuasive if we put our minds to it but it still took a while before we finally convinced the cab driver that honesty really was the healthiest policy. We paid him off and headed for the elevator; next stop—seventh heaven. That's what we thought but we weren't dealing with angels, though they had taken wing by the time we got upstairs.

"They'd taken a few other things too: radio, tape deck, traveler's checks, some cash. I was pissed off, I blamed myself of course. Mac was murderous; he blamed me of course. I thought he was going to have a go at me, he's not exactly big but he's vicious, a typical poisonous Scottish dwarf. Gives no quarter, takes no prisoners. We must have been making quite a row, 'cos the two sleeping beauties in the next room woke up and wanted to know what the hell was going on. So then we had to explain it all to them so that they could yell at the pair of us, though I got the worst of it naturally. Somehow, most of the flak that Mac did get he managed to deflect onto me.

"Once the shouting died down we began to consider what was to be done. There weren't many choices really, we weren't just going to forget it, so that left either calling the police or taking direct action. In other words, there was no choice at all. In short order we were in the street and grabbing a taxi to get us back to the club. On the way we passed the time by telling ourselves what we were going to do to that little pimp when we got hold of him so we were all pretty steamed up when we arrived. We roared into the place like a bunch of berserkers. Looking back, I suppose that wasn't really the best approach. We shouldn't have drawn attention to ourselves so much. We should really have gone in, quietly, looked around, casually, found our man, finally, escorted him outside, tactfully, and kicked the living shit out him. Cheerfully. As it was our feet barely touched the ground. As we burst in through the front door the bouncers and a few of the heftier barflies grabbed us, propelled us across the room and out to the back alley where they proceeded to thump our lights out. Efficiently.

"It could have been worse, I suppose. They could've called the cops on us. They'd have duffed us up and then thrown us in jail. As it was we managed to put up a decent fight and no one got hurt too badly. They got tired after a while and told us to get lost or words to that effect. The rest of us would have been glad of the chance to slink off while we could still walk. Not Mac though.

"'You should buy us a bloody drink after that lot', he piped up. I could see the bouncers were ready to get mean and start over again but one of the punters laughed, he 'admired Mac's spirit.' I suppose I'd admire it too if it didn't get me into so much trouble.

"They wouldn't let us back in the club but the customers took us back to someone's flat and fed us whiskey all night long, real whiskey too. Needless to say, we didn't make the flight the next day, and when we did finally get to the park the weather was socked in solid. It didn't clear up for six weeks, just when we had to leave. Half way around the world for nothing. Didn't even get me leg across."

Seven

Cerro Torre—
Alpine Style
1975

Patagonia is a land where good weather is as precious and rare as water in the Sahara. With rapid weather changes bringing not infrequent 20-or 30-day storms generating winds well over 100 mph, the line dividing a climber's boldness from a climber's stupidity is razor thin. In Patagonia, perhaps, there is no distinction. I questioned from the beginning whether we weren't playing a form of Russian roulette with four chambers loaded. But I had become obsessed with climbing the beautiful tower called Cerro Torre and was prepared to succeed at almost any cost. That's a dangerous frame of mind if allowed to get out of control, but while I was frustrated, I was also determined.

My frustration was rooted in the fact that after a year of organization, preparation, money making, equipment designing, sacrifice, traveling and team selection for this very climb, I had arrived in Patagonia only to have my two partners decide that they had more important business elsewhere. They abandoned me to my own devices. Perhaps it was my resolve to do the climb, perhaps it was the climb itself, perhaps it was my stubborn personality, perhaps there was another reason. But, after traveling all the way from California to Patagonia and seeing the problem in person, so to speak, my two mates decided the weather was better somewhere else. Who knows where the roots of determination are buried? All I know is that I was alone in Patagonia and I wasn't leaving until I got a crack at Cerro Torre.

Sitting alone in Fitzroy Park, surrounded by some of the most scenic mountains on earth, I contemplated a solo attempt on the tower. Then I remembered the young American climber I had met the day before. Steve Brewer had hitch-hiked into the park looking for an expedition to join. I went to him with the proposal of joining my expedition as the other half of a two-man alpine-style attempt on the south-east ridge of Cerro Torre, one of the world's wildest mountains. Without even thinking it over, he agreed. I was given a second chance. At 3:30 a.m. we climbed simultaneously and quickly through the pre-dawn darkness up the lower ice pitches with Steve in the lead. A strong ice climber, Brewer moved methodically upward, placing a token ice screw every 150 feet in order to give me practice in removing them.

Our hope was to reach the lower col by dawn. Caesare Maestri, who has had some experience with the Torre, once wrote, "Hope is a vain word in the mountains." Previous expeditions had placed their advanced snow caves on this col from where they seized the upper ridge. Our strategy was different. We carried the minimum amount of clothing (jacket, pants, sleeping bags), food (oatmeal, sugar, soup), equipment (25 pitons and nuts, 25 carabiners, six ice screws, a small bolt kit, two nine-millimeter ropes) and, of course, courage in our rucksacks. I had spent three years planning this climb, studying photographs and magazine articles and talking with other climbers, designing clothing, doing extensive preparatory climbing, thinking. Nevertheless, I think that if you're not scared, you're not having fun. If that's true, Cerro Torre is worth a couple of years at Disneyland. Treading close to the edge elevates the fear factor, but it also focuses the mind, reducing the possibility of the dreaded slip of attention.

We were vain enough to reach the col half an hour after the sun bathed it in golden light. At 5:30 a.m. I took the lead. The pitches sped by in the blue. Some were pure rock, some mixed rock and ice, some had sections of aid. One nasty, ice-lined 5.10 crack carved its impression into my memory. I drove my ice hammer into its icy depths for a couple of moves until there was no longer anything solid within reach. I was forced, against my peace of mind, to use off-width technique on the quicksilver surface of the interior walls. Going for something that difficult with no protection is called a calculated risk. When I finally reached safety, an eternity later at a loose chockstone, my arms were cramping and I was tired. What has everyone else done here? I asked myself. The mystery vanished when I checked the photo we had brought along, thereby discovering that we were off route. There was easy nailing to the right.

In time, as the climbing and hauling took its toll on my arms, and I was forced to rest. We stopped under a small overhang at the base of a flaring chimney. Above, huge chunks of ice clung precariously to the smooth steep walls. Our tranquility and rest were cut short by the resonant roar of ice rushing towards us. Steve and I smeared ourselves against the wall, molding our bodies to the underside of the overhang. The sky around us became splintered with shattered shards of crashing ice. When the barrage passed the silence was disturbed only by the pounding of my palpitating heart. Ice crystals floated through the brilliant blue sky like tiny winged diamonds, all the richness and wealth we needed at that moment. As soon as the fall ceased I rocketed up the chimney with all the speed and skill at my command. Above hung hungry, threatening, white fangs of ice. There was no telling when something might let go. Swiftly, I reached the safety of a ledge.

I had but a few moments to enjoy safety and contemplate fear. As soon as Steve arrived, I tiptoed across the awful icy slabs on the precarious balance of bolts left by previous explorers. After Steve joined me we immediately began clipping up a long, diagonal bolt ladder toward the ice towers of Cerro Torre in evening light. Bolts or no, I realized that we were higher on Cerro Torre than anyone else had ever been in a single day. I knew that what Steve and I had just done was but a premonition of how fast and well the younger generation will do the difficult technical routes of the future. We had probably made the fastest and farthest progress accomplished in a day on any mountain of that technical standard.

Everything was going according to my plan. Our hopes had been met. Let us re-phrase the great Maestri's words: "Irrational hope is a vain word on the mountains." I thought we would reach the bivouac in the ice towers by dark. Steve graciously and skillfully took over the lead to finish the bolt ladder, giving me, as he always did, a much-needed rest just when I needed it. I led another short line of bolts bypassing a fragile A1 flake. Steve led another pitch, then rappelled back down after fixing a rope. We had climbed 3,500 feet up the Cerro Torre that day. Exhausted and exhilarated, we had to spend another hour and a half chopping a bivouac ledge out of solid ice. We finished excavating at about 11:30 p.m., when we began cooking dinner by headlamp. Eerie orbs of light flashed through the unreal sky, illuminating an icy architecture of surreal but very real surroundings.

Meanwhile, far below, Giuliano Giongo, leader of the Italian Torre Eiger expedition, had his own surreal but real experience. He crawled out of his tent at base camp to see a star sitting on the face of Cerro Torre. He thought his eyes were playing tricks on him. Incredulous, he suddenly realized the star was our headlamp far higher on the mountain than he believed possible. Giuliano called his mates out of their tents to view the rare spectacle.

I woke up periodically during the night to check the weather. The wind had changed and now blew from the west with hints of storm, the inevitable in Patagonia. To be caught in a storm on this mountain would be an ugly situation. No fixed rope. Food for one more bivouac. No bivvy sacks. Only two ropes with us. We had a crucial decision to make.

Dawn arrived with puffy harbingers of an approaching tempest. How much time did we have? We circumvented the problem by ignoring it. Casting our fates to the Patagonian wind, we started racing with the famous predatory weather. Steve cramponed up the ice ridge past abandoned relics of former struggles. Coiled ropes, rack of hardware and carabiners hung from the wall; evidence of other rapid departures. Solid early morning ice allowed us to move swiftly. Confidently, Steve led pitch after pitch, threading his way on the ice between blank pillars of rock.

The high point of the 1971 British expedition was situated 40 feet below a small bolt ladder surmounting a short overhang. At this point the strain of the climb began to show. I dropped my North Wall hammer, and Steve dropped one of his etriers, for which he substituted a couple of slings tied together. From the top of this pitch another bolt ladder led up to the edge of a huge, overhanging tower. I took the lead and had to chop away six to 12 inches of ice to uncover each bolt. Steve dodged the ice I knocked down on him. One more pitch and the final headwall loomed above us, beckoning.

Wispy clouds circled the summit as the weather rapidly deteriorated. Vapory, icy cobwebs moved in many directions at the same time. We clipped up the bolt ladder in unison to speed progress. No doubt most of the headwall could have been aided without the bolts, but it didn't matter since pitons would have been fixed instead.

Menacing clouds swirled everywhere as I climbed past Maestri's compressor, which he had used to bolt his way up. I marvelled at it here near the top of this magnificent spire; getting that hunk of machinery up here was a feat comparable to Hannibal's crossing of the Alps.

Looking up, I saw seven broken bolts leading up and slightly right, but 80 feet of blank granite stretched between the last bolt and the summit snow. My God, I thought, Maestri must have nailed 80 feet of ice tenuously bound to smooth rock. A bad joke, it was inconsistent with the magazine articles. I extracted the small bolt kit and went to work placing aluminum dowels, knifeblades and copperheads. While it seemed slow, Steve boosted my morale by telling me I was moving fast and to go for it. Finally, I could almost touch the ice. After one last copperhead I chopped a groove in an ice-filled crack and placed a Friend. It held and I started free climbing, traversing left with my feet on steep friction with the pick of my hammer in the ice above. I pulled myself onto the summit snowfield. Balancing first on one foot, then the other, I carefully donned my crampons and finished the lead. The summit was an easy walk and I wondered why Maestri and his friend hadn't gone to the top.

Steve came up leaving all the pitons in place. Without stopping, he climbed past me to the summit. Together on top of the ice mushroom, we shook hands and embraced. After taking a few photos, we got the hell out of there. The wind blew at 60 mph on the summit, but eased up 100 feet down. We wasted little time descending, quickly reaching the top of the ice towers. At that point the rappel route deviated from the overhanging climbing route, but it was necessary to rappel straight over the face of those ice-incrusted pillars with the giant, fragile icicle swords hanging on God knows what. Fortunately, we reached the bivouac site without mishap and enjoyed an evening meal of oatmeal and hot chocolate. Storm dragons darted across the maroon and slate-colored sky. Wind is the stalker on Cerro Torre, with the climber a very tiny prey. We were trapped for the night, 3,500 feet above the glacier.

The diffused light of morning confirmed my worst fears. Snow covered everything; the ropes were as stiff as steel cables. We hung up the first two rappels acutely aware in the claustrophobic emptiness of the sound of jet engines mixed with the roar of avalanches. The day seemed surreal yet weirdly familiar, like some deadly dream of deja vú experienced in another life. We finally reached the bolt ladder traverse where we began the slow, methodical task of clipping back down each bolt, reversing the process of only two days before, though it seemed a lifetime ago. I would move 50 feet, then bring Steve down, thus decreasing the immobile period so neither of us would grow too cold.

I clipped into a bolt with a small sling attached to my swami belt, then yelled through the swirling clouds that I was off belay. Suddenly the panic light in my head flashed red. The sling had ripped apart, but I didn't know it yet. I accelerated earthward at an alarming speed. Terminal velocity, no pun intended. This is it, I thought, the last act, just like Toni Egger. My mind shifted into hyper-gear assuming the subtly disconnected viewpoint of spectator. My thoughts were as clear and distinct as a computer read-out. What had happened? What was going to happen? Would I live to see my unborn child? Where is the end of the rope? Would I go all the way to the ground? I heard myself screaming. Shut up, I told myself, screaming doesn't do any good.

Wham! The end of the rope! God, it stretched forever before there was a wrenching jolt as I shot upward like a yo-yo on a string. When I finally stopped bouncing, it took a few seconds to collect my wits which were scattered all over the place. A certain amount of pain speeded reaction time, I quickly yelled up, "I'm OK. Just slipped a bit."

Now that I was responsible for myself again, I had to climb up to get my weight off the rope so Steve could move. I stood on tiny, icy holds, holding on while Steve slid down, fetching my aid slings. It took forever. I had fallen about 120 feet, broken some ribs, chipped an elbow, badly bruised a hip and rearranged my mind. No serious damage, just a great deal of discomfort. Pain is the main thing I remember about the rest of the descent. The endless rappels were fortunately without further incident.

The weather treated us kindly, clearing as we reached the glacier. I stumbled into the Italian glacier camp ahead of Steve where I was warmly received with the congratulations of the exuberant Italians. It was wonderful to hear their praise as they expressed astonishment at the speed of our ascent. "Muy rapido, muy rapido," they exclaimed over and over, speaking Spanish for our benefit. I told them, only half joking, that we moved so fast because we were so scared. Yes, we were pleased with ourselves. Our Italian friends fed us soup and tea with rum for our weary bodies.

Afterwards, I lay on the edge of sleep digesting both the meal and the experience of a lifetime, secure in the satisfying knowledge that we had both met the challenge and prevailed.

Eight

East Face of the Fortress
Epitaph for an Expedition
1988

At 12:32 p.m. on December 6, the Aerolines Argentines flight lifted off the runway at LAX. The 1988 Fortress East Face Expedition was on its way. The last few days had been hectic as is customarily the case. My wife Peggy, bless her, would soon receive the phone bill listing my calls to the necessary sponsors of an endeavor which would bring in no income for the family. I was upset, knowing that I would miss Christmas, an important event when you have a nine-year-old son. Scheduling had no remorse, unlike myself, and this was the necessary time slot. I waited for the 'fasten seat belt' sign to go off and thought about economies to make up the $360 cost of the excess baggage. I wondered why my Italian friends were not manacled by these mundane expenditures. It was the cost of these things that, understandably, dug deepest at my wife. The flight wasn't crowded so, being an experienced flyer, I moved to middle row seats to stretch out and sleep.

On December 7, a warm rain fell on Buenos Aires when Jay, Dave, and I arrived. The next day our plane touched down in Rio Gallegos, where blowing wind and cool rain greeted us. Over the next two and a half days we went on a non stop shopping spree in the markets and shops of this now-thriving town. I talked to the shop keepers in abysmal broken Spanish and discovered that the weather had been very poor for the previous month and a half. This might be good, we agreed. At least we hadn't missed any good weather and the percentages were in our favor for improvement. We arrived early for the bus. Our excess baggage cost the same as two more tickets but at least we now had all of our food.

A change of buses was necessary at the Chilean border. The new bus took us to the Hotel Astral in Puerto Natales. I suspected a set-up—a cousin, sister, or some such connection. Time is of the utmost importance in Patagonia but I cringed when I paid $150 for a personal bus that would take us and all our equipment, off the beaten path of scheduled bus services inside the Torres Del Paine National Park. The saved days of load carries made it an essential expense. It was now December 12 and the longest day of the year would dawn in a little over a week. We looked forward to making good use of it. After arranging for horses which may or may not show up, we packed loads for the next day, just in case.

The next day found us laboring up the 15-mile approach to base camp under 75-pound loads. All this proved too much for Dave's old ski injury. The next day, his very swollen knee put him out of action for we knew not how long. Thankfully, the horses had arrived and were available at the cost of $32 per horse per day as compared to ten dollars at Fitzroy. Yes, Chile was more expensive. We could afford only three horses which could carry no more than 110 pounds each and only up to an intruding moraine. We would have to do the rest. After three more days of shuttling loads, sometimes two per day, base camp was established.

At the lower camp we met some Italians, who were trying to do the North and Central Towers by the easiest routes. They had been fully sponsored including plane tickets. Perhaps we were born in the wrong country for climbers, we speculated. It was decided that divine intervention had kept us poor, or nearly so. Uncooperative weather hindered our efforts to set up advanced base camp—at times it was impossible to reach it. From advanced base camp, three and a half hours of breaking trail up a steep slope of deep wet snow led to the base of the rock. By the second day, equipment and fixing ropes were carried to the base and on the third, Jay and I started fixing pitches.

A large ribbon of ice hung precariously above the climbing route, like a time bomb counting down to an unknown future detonation. After looking the first pitches over, Jay changed into rock shoes, deciding that the climb would be on rock. This was not the case. The tops of surfaces, holds and slopes were invariably coated with ice or snow, and yet, water ran down the rock.

An ice-filled chimney presented a testy problem but Jay utilized a couple of knifeblade pitons for aid. Climbing mostly on rock, Jay persisted leading in rock shoes. We fixed three pitches before increasing wind-driven snow dictated a hasty retreat. By the time we reached advanced base camp, a howling gale was blowing so we continued on down to base camp.

There had yet to be a fine day. Because all our efforts were forced during occasional lulls, we felt reasonably pleased with our accomplishments so far. Rain and high winds kept us at camp, where we made improvements and watched the barometer. We recorded pressure and weather changes to see if a pattern might develop. On Christmas Day we hiked down to the Italian camp, an hour away. To the holiday dinner we brought Dave's homemade bread and other culinary delights. Patagonia forgot it was summer and the barometer fell with a sense of duty. A few days later, brief calm appeared and we ventured up.

Up at advanced base camp, the inclement period had raised havoc. Dave took care of repairs while Jay and I carried more rope and gear to the base of the wall. Breaking trail was the usual exasperating chore. At times we would plunge thigh deep into wet corn snow. The next day Jay and Dave fixed two pitches, the best of the route. There was a catch though—falling rocks. Jay and I had experienced this phenomenon on our previous sojourns in Patagonia. Dave, lacking alpine experience, started looking for small aircraft amongst the clouds. Horrified when he realized the sound wasn't coming from the sky, Dave decided not to return to the wall.

The next day Jay and I went up to fix ropes as far as the top of the snow patch, 1,000 feet up the wall. The temperature had risen, increasing the rain of death to a staccato dirge. We were faced with deciphering between the deadly hum of rocks and the wind whistling through our helmets. The snow field seemed particularly exposed. Missiles were everywhere; no place was safe. The rocks came mostly from the top, and their launch velocity or where they bounced determined their trajectory. We were both concerned, it was a matter of time before one would home in. We descended in worsening weather. It rained that night but cleared in the morning.

A decision had to be made. To continue we had to stay on the wall but there was no safe place to bivouac. Even our hanging tent provided no secure position. Furthermore, from the top of the ropes we could fix, we would need a minimum of three days of reasonable weather to reach the summit. This didn't include getting down. From what we had seen this year and the amount of time left, it was necessary to acknowledge that we were beaten. A miracle was needed and we didn't feel that lucky. We called it quits on the Fortress and sought another objective suitable for an alpine-style attempt. The rest of the day was spent reconnoitering a route on the Central Tower. Jay and I agreed on a line which looked promising and do-able in two days of fast climbing. First, though, the equipment had to be removed from the Fortress. Dave helped us ferry the gear down. That afternoon a storm came in so the next day we scurried to base camp.

Three days passed before we could return. Jay and I spent the night at advanced base camp prior to starting up to the base of the Central Tower under darkening skies. We reached the base after three hours of climbing. After constructing bivvy sites a vigil was kept on the rapidly changing weather. Soon snow joined the violent winds and once again we were forced down. We were unable to get to the base again until a few days later, only to have the same events occur. Base camp was dismal; stress affected all of us. What is the quote? Familiarity breeds contempt. These times tested the depths of a person.

As is sometimes the case, if you think it's bad it can always get worse, which is exactly what the weather did. Still hopeful, we prayed for a break. Let it not be forgotten that before we arrived in the Paine area the weather had been bad for one and a half months so by rights some good days were due. On January 20 it snowed a foot at base camp and the next day it rained as hard as seems possible. With four more days to go before the horses where due, Jay and I still had our gear at the base of the Central Tower. We started to worry about getting it down. The expedition was dead. Time had run out.

Nine

Aquarian Wall
1970

Having decided that it was our turn to be pathfinders, Kim Schmitz and I went snooping around the base of El Capitan late in the fall of 1969, looking for a new route. Armed with high-powered binoculars, we strained our eyes and our imaginations investigating all suspicious wrinkles and folds. Out of four good possibilities, we weeded out all except one. A line that we hoped would not take too many bolts, and which would not be too hard nor too scary.

We chose to name it Aquarian Wall, in line with many traditional route names in Yosemite. At the time we were unaware that only a certain privileged few could name their routes "walls." We were soon informed, much to our surprise, that this route, unlike the North America Wall or the Salathe Wall, was not a wall at all. Certain self-appointed (though inconsistent) guardians of Yosemite climbing traditions strongly urged us to name the route Aquarius. Nevertheless, we stuck by Aquarian Wall, and Aquarian Wall it is, despite what certain people not invited on, nor involved in the climb or its name may say or write.

In deference to our low tolerance for the boring labor of `carpenter' routes (as we referred to those long, uniform crack systems which had to be climbed by repetitious pegging) we decided to immediately explore the tappings on the apparently blank, lower third of the wall. This, we hoped, would provide difficult technical and therefore interesting climbing. Our first attempt would be of an exploratory nature as we planned to return to the project for an all-out assault in the spring during the more stable weather.

Accordingly one sunny morning in late October, we hiked to the base loaded down with all manner of gadgetry. We began nibbling. The immediate goal was a tower at the top of the 900-foot "blank slabs." Although initially they appeared to be blank, we found through extensive inspection, that these slabs had an Achilles Heel. A series of arches offered a practical passage that would require relatively few drilled holes. Kim took the first lead, which looked like a beauty. We avoided a long roof leading off to the right, by nailing a perfect straight-in crack above it that took us exactly where we wanted to go. After a brief section of free climbing followed by a pendulum move, Kim made short work of the easy, but exhilarating crack which traversed above the lip of the roof.

I followed and quickly began work on the next pitch. Quickly describes my work fervour, not my progress. We had assessed this part of the route as difficult and time consuming and unfortunately, this analysis proved to be accurate. All too soon, I found my left hand wrapped around a drill, my right hand beating out a calypso rhythm with the hammer. Our new technology for bolting blank sections of rock used short lengths of aluminum dowel stock hammered into very shallow holes. This technique, developed by the late Jim Madsen, was three times faster than using expansion bolts, but far less secure. So, after judging the likelihood of extreme pegging above, I pounced on the opportunity for some final mental shelter in the form of a solid bolt. Somewhat higher, in a three-inch-wide corner that offered no true sanity or crack, I was pleased with my prudence. I moved cautiously, using small loops of webbing draped over tiny step-like nubbins in the corner. These features soon ended and I began relentlessly beating pitons into the slightest weakness in the blank ripple. After several attempts, the tip of a then newly developed Leeper Z piton just held my body weight. After a few such placements, even this approach proved futile. Once again I was forced to the drudgery of the drill. Using the aluminum technology, this purgatory passed more quickly than expected. My efforts brought me to the beginnings of an arch that widened into the dubious sanctuary of a long, thin, expanding roof. I placed a bolt, together with two pitons, set far apart to absorb and disperse the expansion. After equalizing the tensions on the anchors, I yelled, "Off belay."

Seconding the pitch was an easy task, so Kim was soon at my side, inspecting the anchors. I covered the bolt with my body until his obvious unease prompted me to disclose the missing link in the chain. The short October day soon drew to a close as shadows crept across the Valley floor, calling us down. We filled our water bottles from a convenient spring at the base of the wall, a task we wanted to complete before darkness found us stumbling over boulders en route to my car. The thought of spraining an ankle, or sustaining an even greater injury on the way down was troubling. This would naturally be a cause for suspicion among the local climbing community. Understandably, we were nervous about our first new route on such a big rock. As yet, there were only a handful of routes completed on El Cap, all pioneered by well-known, even famous climbers.

Despite our anxious excitement, we managed a restful sleep. We made a casual departure from camp early the following morning, before many people were about. We reached the top of our three ropes before the sun had turned the sharply etched profile of the Nose. From the belay, I pushed against the haulbag, for additional sideways reach, in order to place the first pin at full stretch. This reduced the chances of expanding the flake, thereby loosening the anchor pins, and seemed a reasonable precaution to take. The roof nailed easily enough, using the standard pin selection of the day. Nuts were not then generally available in this country, and we carried none. The wall above the roof was crackless, but partway along its length, two small wrinkles of diorite rock afforded an exit without my having to drill. It was almost as though they had been made to take a sling in which I could stand. As indeed they were, once I had completed some minor reshaping. Although even after remodelling they were barely adequate, and stimulated tremors in my legs as I drilled as high as I could reach. Later, I would curse my heroics as I had to repeat these maneuvers. Further progress was merely a matter of focusing on the drill bit and puncturing the granite hide of the great stone monolith.

I established a belay station at the base of a thin corner which Kim followed to another short blank wall. We gained height quickly, drilling on the perfectly angled slab. Kim soon pendulumed to easy free climbing across a broken area which led into the base of a corner. I climbed another pitch of crack and chimney as the day drew short. We found a place to hang our hammocks, the old two-point, Mexican beach type. Stringing them between two anchors, we settled in for an uncomfortable night. The western sky provided a stunning sunset punctuated by the glowing edges of cumulous clouds. Soon afterwards, turbulent winds began buffeting our exposed perch. Violent air whipped at us, lifting our bodies and thrashing us against the wall until my tattered hammock shredded. The pride and satisfaction I had felt at having crossed the great slab with only 40 drilled holes disappeared with the zipper sound of nylon rending. Winter arrived with a vengeance after being held at bay by a huge high pressure system that had just passed. In the morning, amid swirling clouds, we roped straight down, drilling anchors on the barren slabs. We were thoroughly demoralized, our spirits broken. Nonetheless, we left two gallons of water at the high point to mark our intention to return in the spring.

We spent the winter ski patrolling at Squaw Valley and enjoying the Lake Tahoe basin of Northern California. Upon our return to the wall the following spring, we reached our high point only to find that the cached water had gone bad. The weather was too hot for big wall climbing during the summer months but even in September, when we returned to our task, we encountered 104 degree temperatures, profaning our resolve and sending us cowering to the ground. We were discouraged. Did the wall have a will of its own and a malicious contempt for our cavalier arrogance? We felt whipped and made the fact known to those eager to usurp our dominion of the route.

Naturally, another attempt was soon under way. This time Rick Sylvester and Jerry Coe were to get a taste of being the water bearers. They fixed two pitches and started up the ropes early the next morning. The skies were graying as we drove down to El Cap in my old '55 Ford to see how our replacements were doing. As soon as we arrived, I put the binoculars to my eyes just in time to see Jerry's lilliputian figure fall from mid-frame to the bottom of the field of view. I turned to Kim, saying smugly, "I guess that pitch is pretty hard." Despite the 40-foot fall on the third pitch, they persevered, spending the night in hammocks at the bottom of the fourth pitch. The second day found them two rope lengths higher. By this time Kim and I were grumbling to ourselves and wishing we were on the wall again. The third day, Rick and Jerry did three pitches which brought them to Timbuktu Towers, but the weather began to deteriorate. The next day, which was dreary and wet, brought the start of rescue operations for two climbers on the West Buttress. Rick and Jerry started rappelling to the ground.

Early next spring, before Kim and I arrived in the Valley, two very good Colorado climbers, Wayne Goss and Jim Logan, attempted the Aquarian Wall; the route was becoming an item. But after reaching Timbuktu Towers they too retreated, mumbling about long reaches and scary aid placements. Sylvester and Coe were making their second attempt when Kim and I showed up. I had broken my arm skiing that spring and was still glumly moping around the meadows, healing and waiting for our chance on the wall. Since Rick and Jerry were a little slow getting started, we told them we intended to have a go at it. Although my arm was still weak, we climbed past their fixed ropes to reach Timbuktu Towers the first day. In passing their high point, we noted an unusual piece of equipment. A fishing pole with a hook attached to one end had evidently been used to reach past difficult aid placements to bolts above. I wondered why anyone would want to be on the climb, yet not want to do the climbing. Had they lost their spirit in exchange for technology?

The next day we nailed the overhanging corner, then with some long reaches, got past a ceiling using only one bolt. The next pitch was a morale breaker. Kim banged his way up a bottomed seam, placing bolts, dowels and pins in an overhanging, leaning corner. We bivouacked at the end of this pitch, our ropes hanging in space as we set up our hammocks. We were sure of doing the wall now since we couldn't possibly retreat; or so we thought. At around midnight I felt the first small drip of rain. Soon the drip became a miniature Yosemite Falls. I spent the most miserable night of my life huddled in my Bat Tent, which was filled with four inches of water.

I didn't dare change position in the night because I couldn't see my hand in front of my face. The next day's slow dawning revealed that it wasn't really raining at all—it was snowing huge white flakes of discomfort. We didn't know what to do and didn't even want to think about it. However, my hands soon became purple and swollen. I shivered uncontrollably, and we had to think about retreat. We decided to nail back down. I threw the haul bag off, but neglected to unclip it. Fortunately the haul line held, as did the anchors. On the second attempt I got the bag to the ground, then jumared down to Kim, cleaning the pitch as I went. One more completely free rappel and we were safely on our way. At the bottom, I kissed the ground and gave thanks to the horizontal.

In late June, good weather and climbing conditions sent us up the wall again. With two pitches fixed, we rapidly climbed to one pitch below our high point, fixed the pitch above and bivvied on a good ledge. Having the bolts and dowels already in place enabled us to make quick work of this section in the morning. The following overhanging pitch, we named the Coral Corner because of the weird calcium formations which ripped apart our hands and clothing.

Kim then dowelled past a large clump of earth and grass to a good crack. The next lead, a giant, left-sweeping bulge, proved one of the most interesting on the climb. Knifeblades, leepers and nested pins led us to the end of the bulge, where we pendulumed off a dowel. Here we entered a large dihedral with easier climbing and raced the shadow of darkness to a good ledge. The wall was alive with El Cap silverfish, many of which met their ends between the wall and our bodies. The next day passed quickly. Two fairly easy, mixed pitches to a giant ledge, followed by three more short ones brought us to Thanksgiving Ledge. We considered a number of choices, all of which looked discontinuous and generally crummy. I climbed a devious and difficult 5.9 A1 pitch and searched for anchors. Every possible placement either expanded or bottomed out. I tried hauling the bag. It swung 60 feet right of the climbing route where it hung up on numerous ceilings. In a blur of obscenities I dropped the haul bag. With only one pitch left to the summit, I decided to traverse across to the West Buttress.

On top at 1 p.m., we waited for some friends who we expected to meet us. After more than an hour, we gave up, hoisted our 70-pound packs on our backs and trudged down the Yosemite Falls trail. To our surprise, we found our friends lounging around back at camp. They hadn't expect us to reach the top for another day, and accused us of speed climbing. If they had spent as much time up there as we had, they too would have wanted to get it over with.

Ten

Shadows
1989

Charlie pulled himself over to the belay station, clipped in and undid his rappel setup.

"You look fried," I said, as he moved around me into his Portaledge. His normal good looks were drawn and grayed with instant age from an extended bout with the toughest of big wall adversaries; the indomitable hammer and drill. "How many holes did you drill?" Charlie swung his legs out over the edge of his new A5 ledge, leaned back against the wall and began removing the fingerless gloves which had been protecting his hands.

"I don't know," he finally replied, having drawn some energy from his brief rest.

"It could be important," I insisted. "We've drilled 35 holes on the last three pitches, broken six or seven drills, placed six expansion bolts, and 29 machine bolts. I was wondering how many we have left, as we're only halfway up this rock."

I had been recruited for this route after the first four pitches had been fixed, and most of the gear carried to the base, what I call a walk-on wall. As a newcomer, I had little knowledge of the amount of equipment available. Charlie's expression betrayed concern as he grasped my point. "The upper sections of this route look a bit sketchy to me," I continued. "It would be embarrassing to run out of drilling gear. We've still just enough rope to reach the ground. I think we should do an inventory in the morning."

After a quick equipment count the following morning, we rearranged the ropes and went down. Pausing part way down the sweeping lower slab, I surveyed our high point on the wall and the route above. The fluorescent pink belay seat, a gift from Crazy Creek, the equipment manufacturers, stood out against the granite like a carbuncle, but the climbing line was invisible without the Palomar telescope.

September rolled by while I worked as a stunt rigger on a movie in New York City. When I returned in October, it was to find the third team member had pulled his gear, having decided that another route looked more appealing. Old friends, Bill Westbay and Cito Kirkpatrick, were visiting the Valley from their native Colorado. When they asked to come along, I said, "Fine, we'll make it a party." Four people seemed like a lot, but when

Charlie and I were last on the wall, it had taken both of us to haul the heavy bag. With a team of four, two could be hauling while the other pair were leading. Days are short in October, so maximum lead time is important.

The weather's moods were schizoid, with storms coming and going like a woman's prerogative. We sat out one short storm on the Valley floor. Normally, this would have been a boring sequence of non-events, but we used the time effectively, by sharpening drills and dialling in the other mundane tasks that complement success. When the clouds parted, allowing the beams of sunlight to burst through, we made a dash for the dome before it could change. In the lead, Billy and I began hoisting the bags already on the wall, while Charlie and Cito manhandled the new additions. Our optimism about leading another pitch that day gave way to realism as the last bag, attended by Cito, came up in the dark. The days were not merely short, but also cold. The sun paid us a brief visit in the late afternoons, unless this sojourn was cancelled by storm clouds marching in from the west and shrouding the face in swirling vapor. I'd experienced this scenario before. The clouds building during the afternoon meant that, in a day or two, rain would start to fall at night or early morning.

Billy led off next morning. An awkward affair, the pitch threaded around and through a series of large, white roofs. As soon as Billy was anchored, I shot up the rope and began the next lead, while Charlie stripped the gear from the pitch below. Rattling flakes led up to a blank section, which I managed to pass, drilling only three holes. Above, an interesting series of discontinuous small corners and thin flakes brought me to a belay, made possible by a couple of good placements, and necessary by severe rope drag. Clouds circling the face accelerated the day's end and the onset of darkness. I slid down the rope to the security of my flat Portaledge and warm sleeping bag, leaving my pitch to be cleaned the following day. By morning the bad weather had receded but still threatened us. Several yards across the wall, a team of park wardens were engaged in some environmental project concerned with peregrine falcons. While Charlie and Cito ascended the ropes, I yelled to Rob, the team leader, and asked for a weather report on their Park Service radio. The prognosis was bad: increasing clouds, bringing snow that night and the next day, snow levels as low as 7,000 feet. Estimating that we were at about the 8,000 foot level, Billy and I began to move our bivouac equipment up under the added shelter afforded by the white roofs. I drilled a line of bolts under the ceilings where Billy had previously used pegs, then began hauling. Billy assured me that my apologies for drilling on his pitch were unnecessary, considering the amount of weight that would be supported on these anchors.

Meanwhile, above us, Charlie slowly made his way across a line of delicate, china-plate flakes, which were hanging tenuously to God-knew-what. At the belay, Cito's teeth chattered enough to wear off the enamel. As I looked down, I saw Rob and `Team Peregrine' prudently fleeing the wall. Our route followed a line up the center of black streaks which marked the wettest part of the wall. Rob and company had been climbing on the white rock, where there were no water streaks. Nonetheless, they were retreating, obviously wiser than us. Clouds thickened around the cliff face, bringing a drop in temperature. The two leaders rappelled down to the new nest, and we all bundled up for the cold night ahead.

The dawn, although still cloudy, brought no snow. Billy shook the cold by cleaning Charlie's pitch then prepared himself to lead the next. We were in the heart of darkness, the blackest rock camouflaged and disguised the thin, flaky features. Mysteries divulged only after the closest scrutiny kept the adventure alive and vital. As we sat below, we could hear the onion-skin membranes of rock on which Billy climbed creak and groan, telegraphing its ominous nature like an African drum in the jungle. In this flaky rock, there was the ever-present fear of a placement expanding the flake without warning, causing the leader to fall. Given our already slow and painstaking rate of progress, any setback could prove disastrous as many pitches remained. With our performance averaging one pitch a day, a long fall could easily mean an extra day on the face—a day of hunger. We burned a lot of calories just to keep warm in addition to those consumed by the physical demands of the climb. Even so, the prospect of having to ration our food loomed as a distinct possibility.

Another uncomfortable night ensued. Except for Charlie, we had all brought along light-weight sleeping bags, which were inadequate for these conditions. In the clear cold morning, I quickly jumped onto the ropes, where stiffness soon fled as warmth crept into my limbs, making me glad that it was my turn to lead. Today was another moving day. While Charlie and I climbed, poor Cito, who hadn't yet had a rest day, helped Billy move the bags three pitches up to our new position. After 40 feet, I found a small ledge that provided an even better bivvy spot, giving them even more hauling. The next pitch took a long, left-facing flake that led toward a long thin roof, and gave access to the upper features of the wall. I liked these thin piton flakes and corners. They represented the last reserves of difficult aid climbing since the advent of copperheads and camming devices.

Half Dome had more of these features than any other rock formation in Yosemite. Like a kid with a big three-dimensional puzzle, I toyed with each piece. Each wafer and plate, scale and slab, was its own separate adventure, until all were linked together. Play ended and work began when blank rock summoned forth the drill. I punched a few holes, placed the anchors, then rapped down while Charlie removed the network of gadgetry.

We slept well that night. I felt optimistic next morning as we were noticeably gaining elevation. Below, I could see Team Peregrine, as well as two other friends starting another new line to the right of Tis-sa-ack. Above in the now crystal clear skies, Charlie drilled the blank section toward the long, horizontal roof. With any luck, we would top out on schedule, in about three days time. The day was still chilly, so Billy and I stayed huddled in our sleeping bags while we took cursory stock of our food supplies. The climbing was going slower than we had hoped, half of the pitch had entailed drilling and the other half had been horizontal. After considerable effort, the height gain had been a meager 60 feet—scarcely a giant step for Mankind.

"We're about four pitches from the top," I speculated.

"That'll mean a day without food, unless we can move faster," Bill added.

Over our heads, Cito swung monkey-like beneath the roof, trying to remove the twin camming devices that Metolius had generously donated. His dedication to the job rewarded by almost total success, only one T.C.U.

was lost when the flake contracted and compressed the cams.

The following morning Billy and I raced up the ropes to get a jump start on the day. Lathered with sweat, I arrived at the high point as Billy finished a rampaging organization of the hardware. We poked and jostled one another on the cramped stance until Billy launched himself onto the next lead. Haste makes waste. He soon plummeted back to earth. Mission Control corrected, and after adjusting his trajectory, he once again pursued an upward course. This pitch ended with some wild steep free climbing to a small, precarious stance which became our next rendezvous. After some interestingly gymnastic cleaning maneuvers, I arrived at the stance and surveyed the next section. It wasn't inviting. We needed to speed our progress but a large, loose flake barred our way and necessitated moving the others up under the roof for safety. The day was too far advanced for such procedures, so we hauled up all the gear not need for the night's bivouac, then descended to join Cito and Charlie.

A noticeable hint of summit fever was in the air as Charlie and I went up to the high point next day. After making sure that the others were safely hidden beneath the overhang, I started work on the extremely loose flake. Even a little weight on the camming device caused it to move an alarming amount. After some internal debate, I let the drill do the talking. One quick hole sufficed, then I hooked across the top of the flake. Once safely above the precarious monstrosity, the climbing became interesting and challenging. I climbed to the last remnant of rope, pitying Charlie as he came up to discover yet another large section of blank rock. He'd had all the big blank sections and I felt sorry for him, though not enough to change his fate. The remainder of the day was filled with the cheery sound of Charlie at work, broken only by brief inquiries from us about the distance to the top. The summit overhangs were now in sight, clearly but a short pitch above the end of Charlie's labors. This, of course, was not the case. When Charlie completed his lead, Billy began the final `short' pitch to the summit. Only after several tremendous reaches through the overhangs and 165 feet of tightly stretched rope, he stood on top shortly after dark. We slept on the crown of the great dome, reserving the last morsels of food for the morning. The rest of the day was spent in cleaning up the garbage we had dropped as well as more that the American Alpine Club had overlooked on their clean up just two days earlier. We loaded the cars at dusk and went in search of food.

Eleven

Reservations
1977

On a clear, beautiful night typical for Yosemite in the summer, a few of us sat around camp hanging out at the local bar. Pull-up bar that is, pumping a few reps to work off an overdose of Lodge coffee. A passer-by, drawn by the activity, strolled into our small conclave to see what the haps were. It turned out to be an old compadre from out of state who I hadn't seen for more than a year. He looked a little the worse for wear and was, he said, working off an overdose of another sort himself. In between our bar sessions he related his exploits during his absence. When his narrative swung to taboo desert towers, he captured my attention for I had longed to tread their summits myself.

"The Totem Pole," I said in amazement, almost mimicking his words as he began to tell the tale of his most recent adventure. I hung on Jeff's every syllable as this was a desert classic which I prized above all others. He wove a wicked yarn that garnered people to him wherever he went. I admired his gift of gab and locked myself to a wooden bench for the free entertainment.

Jeff hacked a smoker's cough, cleared his throat, and began.

"'Benny,' I said, 'we gotta go do it man. It's like a stone pencil teetering on the brink of disaster and we gotta do it before it falls over like the Gendarme in Seneca. We're so close here in Flagstaff, man—half a day away. We'll hate ourselves if we pass up this chance.'

Benny's a Scandinavian dude: real stubborn. He'd heard all the scuttlebutt about the injuns not diggin' the white man an' climbers an' all and he's like, WHITE. I mean he stands out around dark folks like ink on a white shirt. So he's real paranoid when it comes to tribal lands. One thing the red man and blockheads got in common though, is a genetic response to firewater. A few shots of vodka or better yet, ice cold aquavit and I'm an alchemist buyin' Valhalla with a few beads. So I buy a big bottle. He takes the bait and slicker than snot on a hand rail, I got him in his orange beater Datsun while he was still a Viking and grabbed a couple sixers of road pops for the come down.

"The only bad part was Benny had to drive. M.A.D.D. would have been more than a little pissed off to see us couple of yahoos barreling down the boulevard. We were on a mission from Thor with Benny at the helm. I'd created a monster. Benny was pretty good at drivin' for a man almost legally dead. He dodged and weaved his way through unseen adversities while somehow keeping at least two wheels on the road. I knew though, if I didn't get him out of the driver's seat my hair would be the same color as his before the odometer cranked over another mile, so I was poppin' and pourin' cold ones down his gullet to get him to pull off for a nature break. I hoped it would happen before another car came the other way and reported us to real people.

"Nature prevailed. The door flew open and Benny emerged from the car in a cloud of dust caused by his swerving skid to the road shoulder. Staggering, he fell over and rolled down the road bank with his pants undone and I took command. When he crawled back to car he didn't notice he wasn't driving. Praise the Lord, I might not need Grecian treatment after all. Soon Benny's robust snoring was filling the car with firewood and obscuring Led Zeppelin on the tune box."

Jeff lit a smoke for effect, looked around to see if everyone was properly riveted, and once satisfied continued.

"The orange Nippon beater rolled into a two-horse town just outside of Indian lands before Benny lived again. I got out to fill-er-up while Benny tumbled out the other door in urgent search of the toilet. When none appeared he slipped around the back, awakening the scrutiny of the huge Navaho station attendant. I pumped the gas as the Indian's perpetual scowl soured even more when Benny reappeared, still buttoning his 501 Levis. Stuffing the piece of old plaid shirt where the gas cap had once been, I hurried back in to pay Cochise. Benny poked his head in as the cash register jingled to ask in affected English where we could buy beer. If looks could kill, we'd have been ant food. Without speaking, the huge red man pointed down the road with a curt movement of his furrowed chin. Not pressing further, we clattered down the road in the appointed direction. With a warning from the store proprietor about alcohol on Indian reservations, Benny took the helm and headed toward Monument Valley Indian Reservation. Benny and I tried to dispose of the illicit liquid before entering intolerant territory but familiar landmarks started to appear long before the 12 pack disappeared, despite Benny's dedication. We made the turn and bounced down the dirt switchbacks to the totem pole." Though entertaining in itself, Jeff's story gained interest as the tale drew closer to that forbidden spire of red sandstone. I could clearly picture the two of them crazed with alcohol and more than likely other controlled substances, as yet unmentioned, hell bent for a Navajo jail. They say God protects crazy people and I wondered if they might make the cut.

Jeff fished a glowing coal out of the fire, bare fingered, and lit another cigarette, then took a drink from a dubious water bottle lined with algae. This relic had been gathering dirt under the table since the last big wall. Without wincing, he continued.

"We roared into the viewing area, quickly followed by a billowing cloud of dust that trailed the Toyota. An annoyed tourist turned to glare and cough at our arrival. The car shuddered to a stop amid the other vehicles. Taking little notice, I lit a cig as Benny popped open another beer with apparent indifference to local laws restricting alcohol. Soon one by one, the tourists departed in disgust, revealing an array of thick wooden signs all of which started with the word No: No

Camping, No Hiking, No Overnight Parking, No Climbing, No Private Vehicles Beyond This Point. Before I could finish perusing the negative messages, the orange Toyota sputtered to life. I ran for the open passenger door just as wild-eyed Benny locked it into gear. I dove onto the exposed springs of the tattered seat as the little car launched toward a breach in the signs where a sandy four-wheel track headed out in the direction of the stone phallus. The door slammed automatically behind me from the velocity of the car. Away we went like escaped convicts, bouncing over the drifted sand.

"After a few hundred yards I thought we might make it but just then the car started to bog down as the road rose gently. Benny punched it. The engine screamed and the tires spun, making furrows in the soft red dusty mire. Hope waned as the r.p.m.s dropped and the old battered car settled into the sand with a shudder. Sheep-eyed, Benny turned to me. I opened the door, neglecting a response in his direction, and stepped out to assess our predicament. It didn't take rocket scientist to see we were fucked. Buried to the frame, the wheels still spun slowly with the car in gear. Finally Benny got out of the car like a puppy that had been scolded for shitting on the rug. Slowly he came around to my side.

"'Did I fuck-up Jeff?'" he whimpered.

"'What the hell do you think? You Viking cretin! Look where we are, you blockhead, Benny. We're in plain view of anyone at that pullout. You think they'll see us? Oh no, only if they look toward the Totem Pole. We stick out like a sail on the ocean. Of course they can see us. We can see them, can't we? We're a damn bust sittin' here. We're talkin' BIG fines, jail time, climbing gear, an' car gone. Get the photo, Benny?'"

He sulked then asked, "What do we do, Jeff?"

"'Well, fortunately it's late and maybe nobody will show up till morning, which may give us ALL night to get this damn piece of junk out of here."

Jeff became very animated now as his story progressed. The group hung on his every word. Jeff still had his hair so we knew he and Benny escaped, but how? Jeff continued.

"I told Benny to collect sagebrush. It sounds easy enough, but there were scant amounts to be found in the vicinity. After a while we had enough, and stuffed it behind the rear tires. Benny got in the driver's seat and I pushed. We traded off but after an hour of repeated vein-popping efforts the car was only 40 feet closer to a dry wash where it would be hidden. Now the orange heap was thoroughly entrenched. We collapsed in the sand exhausted. We sat there, staring at the car and drinking beers, when out of the blue a white, four-wheel drive car pulled into the viewing area.

"Benny," I said, "let's run back there and see if we can get those people to tow us to the dry wash. If we could get the car there we can turn it around on the firm ground, then get some speed up to drive it out." Quaffing down the beers, we took off at the closest we could come to a run. Huffing and puffing, we arrived at the viewing area to discover the occupants of the white vehicle were two attractive German girls apparently touring the natural wonders of the U.S.A. Listening to bits and pieces of indecipherable dialogue, Benny and I turned to each other and smiled, our fiendish hormones oozing. Benny's a big kinda guy, with good-looking Germanic features and a nearly white mat of hair. So I says to Benny, "'You fit with them better than me, get over there and chat these gals into rescuing us."

"Benny squirmed.

'What should I say?'

He had a point I thought. Looking at the signs all beginning with NO and then looking out at the car in obvious violation of one sign, its windows reflecting the setting sun, conversation could be awkward to say the least. What should he say? Oh, we can't read or we don't give a damn about rules? It wasn't that we were tongue-tied when it came to talking to women. Drinking this much beer we could have talked with the Queen of England, but our brains were a little slow at coming up with an acceptable line of bull. Soon it was too late. The girls got back into the four-wheel drive "tow truck" and slowly drove away as we watched stunned and abashed at our idiotic ineptitude. I walked over to the sign that said No Private Vehicles Beyond This Point, hung my hands over it and gazed at the forlorn little jalopy. How appropriate. We shuffled aimlessly back without a plan. We reached the car, opened the doors, plugged in a Hendrix tape, flopped in the sand and started killing off the rest of the beers. That way we wouldn't be busted for having alcohol on the reservation; a convenient rationale. Two beers later Benny suggested a desperate plan: Abandon the car, take the license plates and registration, put everything into our packs and escape like fugitives.

"'Absolutely not!' I snapped, 'We've got all night to move this piece-of-shit car 300 feet and we don't quit 'till then. But still neither of us moved. After a couple of silent minutes, I stated what seemed the truth.

"What we need is a miracle, an act of God."

"Benny laughed, 'Yah sure.'. Ten minutes later it started to rain. It was almost like a direct dial to the big guy. We had hope. Rain would settle and consolidate the sand. Getting a second wind, we started digging the sand from under the car. The rain stopped but then I suddenly got an idea.

"'Come on Benny,' I said 'I got a plan. Grab some wrenches and a screw driver.' Benny isn't usually a total hammerhead. I had sandbagged him and the inertia had taken over from there. Besides being an adroit climber, he's a pretty sharp guy in general. He knew right away what my plan was. We took off for the viewing area. Once there we commenced removing the signs from their upright posts. Leaving the nuts and bolts on top of the posts, we returned to the car with the tools for our escape. It took a little while to dig the sand from under the car and position the signs in troughs dug behind the rear tires, but when it was done we knew it was going to work. Taking turns as before, one pushing and one driving, we made a game of it. When it was my turn to drive it was my lead, like in climbing, and the same for Benny. The idea was to see how far you could move the car during your lead. Even with the help of the signs, it took more than four hours to move the car the 300 feet to the drywash where it was hidden from view. It was 11 o'clock and long after dark. We celebrated with the last beer and walked back to replace the signs before anyone noticed. Pulling our sleeping bags out, we threw them out on the sand with hopes of still climbing the Totem Pole. Within minutes we were comatose.

But not for long. Splat, splat, pitter-patter, pitter-patter. Rain, once our saving grace, was now our nemesis to much-needed sleep. Sure, it would make the track more passable tomorrow, but it played hell with getting any sleep now. Benny curled up in the front seat of the car, cramped at best, while I persisted in the sand. The rain stopped but started again with a vengeance. Benny honked the horn for me to come to the car. I flopped into the other front seat, soaked and coated with sand. A scorching desert sun drove us out of the car after a completely miserable night.

"Exhausted, we threw some gear together and straggled up to the base of the climb. The new route was on the back side away from the viewing tourists and monument police. The subterfuge of this route was complete, except from wandering sheep herders who could divulge our dissident behavior to the police. I tossed a coin and drew the first of three leads. Using camming devices, the climbing went quickly and in total silence until the final headwall. Here two pitons had to be placed in bolt holes where the bolts had fallen out. Not uncommon in the soft red sandstone. I flattened myself as I pulled onto the summit to avoid being seen and waited for Benny. Together on top at last, we slithered like reptiles to arrange the ropes for the rappel. Using Ninja stealth, we slid from the summit without a snag. On the ground we scratched our heads when we realized it had taken a little more than three hours to do the 450-foot spire and five and one-half hours to move the car 350 feet the evening before. Benny and I hopped in the little Japanese gem and drove it out. A clean get-away for the bad guys.

"All you bros are probably wondering if it was worth the trouble," Jeff exclaimed.

"Yeah dude, it sounds like a total epic bummer," someone in the darkness said.

"Was it really worth all that?" chimed in another Californian. There was a long pause while Jeff stoked up another smoke, then finally drawing on his cig he slowly shook his head.

"Nope."

Twelve

Nose in a Day
1975

On June 21, 1975, Billy Westbay, John Long, and myself, strode toward the great, sweeping south buttress of El Capitan, commonly called "The Nose." In the pre-dawn hours the full moon illuminated all its colossal splendor. Could we climb it in a day? We thought so. But to tell the complete story of this fleeting moment of glory I must shackle past memories and go back to a time before John or Billy had even seen El Cap, let alone climbed its glacier-buffed stone. The historic first ascent, with its tenacious heroics and creative ingenuity, is well documented. So too, is the first continuous ascent from the ground up. But few people perhaps no one other than myself, is familiar with the original seeds that gave rise to the idea for the first one-day ascent.

There was a man, but more so, there was a spirit in the form of Frank Sacherer. Had anyone but Sacherer said "I want to do the Nose in a day" the response from any Camp Four regular would have been incredulous laughter. But Frank frequently accomplished what others thought impossible. He had climbed free, routes that the best climbers of the day said couldn't be done free. He had climbed in a day, routes they said could not be climbed in a day. In a word Frank Sacherer was visionary. The driving force of climbing in the 1960's, he did more to advance free climbing as we know it today than any other single person in America at that time. During the summer of 1965, Frank and I made a reconnaissance of the Stoveleg Cracks on the Nose to see if they could be climbed free. These wide cracks were so named from the homemade pitons, fashioned from the legs of old stoves, used to aid these cracks on the first ascent. Frank thought that if this section went free, then the Nose might go in a single day. Preposterous: but Frank hated camping on the walls and for him the Stoveleg Cracks were the key. In 1966, work on his physics thesis pre-empted all climbing activity. By 1967 his research work had taken him to Geneva, Switzerland.

This left me to accept the challenge and carry the torch. In pursuit of the goal I set out in June of 1967, with my friend and trusty belayer, Jim Stanton, hoping to climb the Nose and at the same time attempt to free climb the Stovelegs. With ropes fixed as far as Sickle Ledge we charged the wall in classic Yosemite fashion—after a leisurely breakfast. A casual approach, yes, but at the time, I was primarily interested in freeing the

Stoveleg Cracks not on speed records, hence a coffee-shop start. Stanton, a gnome-like person, had never climbed a grade six, let alone El Capitan, but then I had yet to climb the 'Big Stone' myself. By 1:30 p.m. I'd freed the Stovelegs and we were on our way down. A water bottle cap had broken as the result of the haulbag swing into the corner above Dolt Tower. Everything in the bag was now soaked, and we were a gallon of water short. The mishap had occurred because the bottle had been packed sideways in the bag, making it more vulnerable. Returning to El Cap the next afternoon, we completed the route in two days.

Eight years passed. Other climbs, mostly first ascents, took precedence over climbing the Nose in a day. But in the spring of 1975, I had some new thoughts and feelings about climbing; alpinism beckoned me to new adventures. Speed was, I felt, the key to safe alpine climbing. Climbing the Nose in a day offered a good test of speed-climbing abilities, so I started rounding up suitable personnel. The bar was a good place to stimulated interest and to polish the luster of the Nose project and a few climbers had blossomed into likely candidates. Of those, I had selected two the previous year and sewn seeds to motivate them. I refreshed their enthusiasm in the bar before going south for two weeks to give a climbing demonstration for the Navy S.E.A.L.s. I knew I wouldn't have time to get in good condition before returning, so I wanted to be sure that they were. I hoped they would make up for any deficiencies I might have.

Just as I'd expected, climbing with the S.E.A.L.s proved to be no cakewalk. I had to set up topropes, give demonstrations of technique, and deliver lectures. After all that, the boys wanted to take me out on the town until three in the morning. America's best had unusual training habits. I deduced that they were getting in shape to stay up long hours with little sleep, then mobilize with hangovers. Maybe they were training for high-altitude climbing.

The Valley of Light provided a welcome sight when I returned. Though the S.E.A.L.s were durable, could they climb the Nose in a day? I wondered now if I could. The longest day of the year, less than a week away, coincided with a full moon, making this the perfect opportunity. I had little time to get in shape. We did manage one ten-pitch training climb, then spent a day rehearsing each of our individual pitches as far up as Sickle Ledge.

Our logistical plan was my responsibility and, I hoped, well thought out. We would take three nine-millimeter ropes of questionable vintage but the best I had. In addition, we carried: 25 nuts, 25 pitons, (camming devices didn't then exist) and one and a half gallons of water. I would lead two of the four pitches below Sickle Ledge with John and Billy taking one each. Above Sickle, John would lead as far as Boot Flake as his big hands were most appropriate for the predominately large cracks through this section. Billy drew the middle part of the route which was mostly mixed aid and free climbing. An excellent free climber from Colorado, he was used to switching from aid to free and vice versa. I had the anchor leg from Camp Five to the top. We would all be tired by then, so aid climbing would probably be the technique of choice. Because of years of practice had honed my nailing skills, I was the natural candidate for the position. I had worked out a system whereby the person leading trailed one free rope and led on another, which he clipped through the gear. Once the rope was anchored, the second man removed the gear, while the third man ascended the leader's trail rope on jumars, as fast as he could, towing the remaining rope. When the third person reached the belay he exchanged the ends of the ropes with the leader, who then charged off on the next pitch. Theoretically this procedure left time for the leader to have a cigarette and to light another for the belayer when he arrived. With 34 pitches to climb, we required a pack and a half of cigarettes each because we all smoked.

The night before the climb, we feasted in the restaurant, then went to the bar for a beer to calm our over-active nerves. At 9 p.m. we retired to my girlfriend's dormitory room where we set the alarm for 2 a.m. before settling down for an all-too-brief sleep. I blinked and the alarm went off. In unison we sprang out of bed, whipped up a giant batch of omelettes, wolfed them down and marched to the car while taping our hands for climbing. At 4 a.m. the moon was bright enough to read by, so we didn't need our headlamps.

As we had already rehearsed the first four pitches, we galloped off, having memorized every move and every nut and pin placement. As the night waned, we reached Sickle Ledge where John and I changed places on the ropes. Away he went. Pitches rolled by like dollars on a New York taxi meter. John flew up the Stoveleg Cracks with the certainty of the Yosemite veteran that he was, reaching the top of Dolt Tower by 6:15. Here, our clamor roused two bivouacked climbers from their slumber. Bleary-eyed one asked where our haul bag was. I responded by pointing to a small rucksack on my back. His expression became quizzical as he looked at our bizarre style of dress. In our purple and pink doubleknit pants, worn with paisley and African print shirts, we presented a questionable apparition to any eyes, sleepfilled or otherwise. Our inspiration for this colorful display was a magazine cover photo displaying several British climbers dressed in traditional, conservative guide's sweaters and knickers, all of the same color and style. The group formally posed with the Eiger looming in the background. As a joke we decided to represent the non-traditional Yosemite avant garde.

Due to the popularity of the Nose route, we had anticipated many obstacles on a one-day ascent: passing other parties on the climb. We were lucky to pass the only party on the route with ease.

John efficiently lowered off the corner of Dolt ledge and ran the rope to the next belay, clipping a solitary old expansion bolt en route. Free climbing the Stovelegs had become commonplace, but John's disregard for protection departed from normal form to meet the demands of speed. He'd been training for this climb and displayed a well-oiled performance. I was less honed and my arms were beginning to cramp with the torrid pace. So far our time schedule hadn't been affected by me, but I was concerned that my performance might be a factor late in the day. It seemed only minutes before John was clipping the bolts toward Boot Flake, four pitches higher. This was his thirteenth lead, not including the fourth-class pitch up the Sickle. Without hesitation, he launched straight into a committing lieback from the final bolt of the ladder. As Billy and I watched from Texas Flake, we hadn't a clue that his arms too were cramping. In silent despair, he hung from a failing hand jam. with the last of his strength, he wedged a hexcentric nut into the crack, clipping into it just in time and averting an 80-foot airball. Between great, heaving gasps, he explained his near-circus performance.

The game plan dictated a change of leaders at this stage anyway, apparently none too soon. Billy jumared the free rope, trailing the third as I cleaned Boot Flake. Without going to the top of the Boot, Billy began the spectacular pendulum known as the King Swing. He was successful on his first attempt, with John and me in hot pursuit. The climbing changed at this point from the straightforward cracks, so typical of Yosemite, to less obvious, circuitous climbing, reminiscent of his home turf in Colorado. Billy proved to be the right man for the job as he flowed up the pitches with fluid ease. Reminiscent of the Flower Tower, the Great Roof grew rapidly closer as pitches scrolled by successively.

Our haste was not unchecked, however. The trail rope jammed in a crack without our noticing until it came tight on the still-leading Billy. A lost rope would be disastrous. Murphy's Law was in effect, as always, and we should have been paying closer attention. We managed to clear the snag within a couple of minutes, and Billy continued. at 1:30, we reached Camp Four, where we enjoyed a welcome five-minute break. To qualify as a one-day ascent, we had to complete the route within 24 hours, a feat which now seem assured. Failing a natural disaster, like the axis of the earth shifting, we would be well within the required time frame.

At the Great Roof, I lowered John out and across the void until the rope ran straight up to Billy, stationed at the belay some 50 feet to the right. I waited for him to gain some altitude and then let go of the rope. True to form, the unexpected occurred. The rope whipped across and made a perfect hitch around horn of rock as though its malicious intelligence was just waiting for an unwitting mistake like this. John roared like a wounded buffalo when the rope halted his progress. It stretched like a tuned guitar string between his waist and the horn of rock. As he pulled on the rope with his Herculean arms, the horn shuddered, then lifted off, a launched missile headed for space. The afterburners misfired and the projectile fell toward two unsuspecting climbers below. I screamed, "Rock, rock," then prayed for the best and continued cleaning the pitch.

By 3:00 p.m., we had reached Camp Five, and I took over the home stretch. It was obvious that someone had recently taken the time and effort to remove all the fixed pitons from the route. I'd been on a rescue in these upper dihedrals the previous year, and they had been festooned with fixed gear. Stripped of hardware, these corners would now be slow going. Speed in aid climbing is a product of efficient movement, the avoidance of errors, and not falling. With these things in mind I went as fast as I could. Some of the pitches were predominately aid while others I climbed partly free. John spurred me on: "Hurry man, we gotta make it down before the bar closes." Inspired by such encouragement, I combined two pitches into one. A rope got stuck in a crack but John freed it. Then, without warning, I dropped an aid sling. As it plummeted through space, I yelled out instinctively. Billy, as though it was routine, reached out and grabbed it in mid-flight.

The summit overhangs suddenly appeared as I turned a slanting corner and I remember wanting to just keep climbing but I knew we would have to belay once more. I waited impatiently for perhaps a whole five minutes for John to reach my side then started the final bolt ladder to the summit. I couldn't help but notice how much the bolts had deteriorated in the seven years since my last passage here, and I wondered how much longer this silent monument to Warren Harding's tenacity would endure.

All things must pass and so did this day. We stood on top at 7:00 p.m. Allowing little time for elation, the three of us took off at a run down the East ledges. My shoes, already killing my feet, soon filled with sand and small stones to add to the torment. Just as my feet hit the pavement of the road the evening turned to night, and the moon shone the great stone as we strode to the car. It was a long way to go in a day. Friends met us outside the Mountain Room Bar with a heros' welcome. Soon, I had more drinks in hand than I could juggle. My fondest memory occurred the following day when Warren Harding, the man who had pioneered the Nose and El Capitan, gave me his warm congratulations. I thanked him and hobbled toward the cafeteria for some stolen coffee.

Thirteen

The Grand Master
1973

W ho's the old dad sitting by the window?" Al asked. "He looks kind of familiar."

Jesse stopped gazing at his nearly flat Budweiser long enough to glance across the barroom to where a craggy, elderly man sat framed by a picture window. Outside, mixed rain and snow fell with dismal vigor, clinging fitfully to the trees and creating a drab, wintery backdrop.

"Mmm, not sure, but I've seen him around before." Jesse mumbled pensively. "Drake might know, he's in his thirties he could probably tell you if ya really got a thing about it."

Al gave Jesse a curt look. With a finger-snap of impatience, he turned to look for Drake, who was where he had been for the last hour. Dressed in cut-off shorts and a 'muscle shirt' despite the late autumn chill, with his arms folded across his chest (to emphasize his bulging biceps), he leaned against one of the pillars that held up the round metal chimney over the fire place. As usual, no fire burned in the dusty grate. Al started in that direction but wondered if he should interrupt Drake's intense sell-job on the good-looking tourist dolly who simpered and preened in the warm glow of his eager attention.

He skirted around so as to approach from the flank. For an older guy, Drake was still competitive material with the ladies. Al, at 20 years of age, was as gawky and sensitive as an adolescent. He felt a little handicapped around women, but hopeful. With considerable tact for a young climber, or indeed any climber, he waited for the right moment before commandeering Drake's attention. He spoke softly, glancing towards the athletic, grey-haired man by the window.

"Say Drake, do you know who that old guy is, the one sitting on his own over there?" Drake's arm shot aggressively towards the youth. Shit, thought Al, I should never have used the word old, stupid. The thought rang in Al's head as Drake started stabbing him with sharp verbal abuse until, realizing that he was blowing the scene with the babe, he detuned his attack. He flashed a quick smile at her which she returned with a frosty display of tombstone teeth. As Drake took Al aside, the lad was already trying to repent, but the older man ruthlessly overrode him.

"Old is in your mind, kid. Some people are over the hill at 20." Drake, well aware of Al's age, gleefully used the knowledge to underscore his point. "That dude may have some greys and he may not be snappin' on the 5.14's, but he'd tear you a new asshole in the mountains. He's forgotten more about climbing than you'll ever know!" Drake's voice was picking up volume. Al knew how Drake liked cliches, so with tolerance beyond his years, he waited for Drake to get around to answering his question in his own abusive way. Finally Drake ended a lengthy recital of feats and first ascents that sounded like a mythical resume spiced with a dash of idolatry. Al shrugged.

"So?"

"What do you mean, so?" Drake spluttered.

"So, what's his name?"

"I thought you would have guessed by now, but I forgot, you kids only read about training techs and last week's firsts," he continued as Al cringed under the withering scorn. After pausing for effect, he announced: "Josh Niles."

"Really!" As Al's mouth formed a perfect 'O' of awed recognition, his attitude changed from indifference to something approaching diffidence.

"You think, like, you could introduce me?"

"I've only talked to the guy once or twice, I don't really know the dude." Drake's bluster left him abruptly and he sounded apprehensive. Most of his friends have quit climbing or are probably dead, he thought to himself. "Yeah," he said aloud, "He might not mind the company. I don't think I want to meet her husband anyway," he confided with a sly glance at the gold band adorning the slim finger of Drake's erstwhile prey. Her gaze, in any case, had already begun to wander now that she was no longer the center of anyone's attention.

Jesse shook his long blond hair out of his face as he watched Drake saunter across to the window table, Al trailing half a step behind. As they introduced themselves, the man half stood to shake their hands, indicating with Old World courtesy that they should join him at the table, which seated four. The waitress, with calculating greed, had already tuned in to the possible sales opportunity of the soft-spoken, older man.

"So then, Mr.Niles, sir," Al began with a note of genuine respect, almost reverence, in his voice. Josh let the formal protocol float despite his distaste for it. Yet another reminder that he was older, with a time limit waiting out there. He saw things differently from these youngsters. How few others could relate to his feelings, even among his contemporaries; those still living. He still felt like an outsider in these situations, like a novel oddity, but he had learned to cope gracefully.

"Do you mind telling me a little about Patagonia?" Al continued. "I want to go down there this winter and I know you've been there a lot." He lied about knowing but threw it in to seem more knowledgeable.

Fatherly notions and emotions filtered through Niles's mind for an instant but his expression didn't change. "Well..." he began just as the pretty cocktail waitress appeared.

"May I serve you gentlemen something?" she bubbled with pert coyness to Josh, who smiled slightly as Drake jumped brashly on the opening.

"Yeah Lisa, got any 'cock'-tails?" he asked, crudely emphasizing the first syllable. She ignored Drake's pointed and unsubtle humor.

"Wait your turn Drake, I was asking the gentleman." She emphasized 'the gentleman,' extracting her small revenge.

Al, meanwhile, was deaf to the trite reparté. He waited politely for wisdom to spring forth from Mr. Niles, who after ordering drinks, became pensive. Leaning back in his chair he crossed his elegantly clad legs. The expensive pants, like his designer sweater, were sponsor's freebies, remnants from expeditions past. He regarded Al thoughtfully for a moment before speaking.

"So you want to go to Patagonia. What did you have in mind, Al?" he said, using his name to ease the boy's tension, which he now found amusing. It was a loaded question, a test. What did the kid know, if anything?

"Well, I'd like to do a couple of big new routes," he blurted out, his enthusiasm overcoming his shyness. "I can climb easy 13s and I've done a lot of A5s too." Al was anxious to impress Mr.Niles and it was, after all, no more than the truth. An understanding smile flitted across Josh's features.

"Well" he said, thinking how contradictory '5.13' and 'easy' were, that type of talent is certainly nice to have, but more than likely it won't come into play."

"Why's that?" the youngster asked with honest puzzlement.

"I guess you could say the most important skills would probably be acknowledged with some embarrassment these days." Without being able to escape the fact Josh knew he'd just dated his climbing career and likewise himself. He still had considerable technical skills but had no illusion about comparing himself to those 20 and 30 years his junior. Others now thought of him as a 'Grand Master' which he rather liked.

"What sort of skills?" Al broke into Josh's reverie.

"Mixed climbing for speed, mainly, and just like any skill it takes practice. You need to practice climbing fast, not fancy. I can't exaggerate the importance of speed. You'll have maybe two consecutive days of good weather, probably only a day and a half, so once you embark on a route you have to get to the top and back down as quickly as you can. But first you can forget all about the arguments you guys are always getting into about ethics. Down there we're talking about survival—ethics get blown away with the wind. When that wind threatens to shred the clothes off your back while you watch rime building up on your rope as well as on the rock and you're 5000 feet from the living, why then, 5.13 and all that tends to lose importance, if you get the picture."

Their mouths dropped in unison.

"Wow!" Al blurted, "Yeah, I see what you mean. That sounds radical, but the purists would still shoot you these days."

Lisa came with the drinks, two Buds for the boys and a hot Grand Marnier, in its appropriate snifter, for Josh.

"You can keep your cold beers. This is the ticket for this weather." He inhaled the warm fumes appreciatively, cupping the bulbous glass in both hands.

Jesse, who had been watching the group with mounting interest, could control his curiosity no longer. Pausing at the bar to renew his drink, he made his way over to the table.

"Hi Drake, what's happening?" and to Josh, "Hello sir, my name's Jesse—Jesse James."

Niles took Jesse's outstretched hand. "Hello there, call me Josh."

Jesse grabbed the remaining chair and perched sideways on it, one arm resting along the backrest. Josh continued where he had left off.

"I suppose I could labor the point but when you find yourself in that position you'll get the idea soon enough." Jessie was immediately lost but Josh didn't go back to fill in the blanks. "There are other physical talents, like tolerance for pain and suffering. But you don't practice those until the need arises, it's like hitting your thumb with a hammer if you follow me." A veteran of the lecture circuit, Josh knew when to pause for laughter as he did now, using the moment to sip contentedly at his drink. As the liquor warmed his stomach, so he warmed to his theme. Visibly relaxing, he continued.

"The mental skills are more tenuous, and harder to learn. For example, the ability to just hang out during the bad periods without losing patience yet still maintaining your focus. That way you can come off the sofa, so to speak, when the weather window opens up.

"What are ya talkin' about ?" Jessie interrupted, frustrated.

"Patagonia," Al answered curtly. "But what's it really like? My bros, I mean my friends, mainly they said it was really awesome."

"That's a good description," Josh conceded, "but maybe somewhat simplistic for the truly inquisitive."

"Huh!" Jessie exclaimed. No one he knew expressed themselves quite like that.

"So you want the whole gig laid out?" asked Josh, slipping into the vernacular, thereby dating himself once again. Jessie looked relieved.

"Yeah, could you tell us what was it like in the old days, I mean ..... before," he concluded in an apologetic tone.

"Sure, if you don't mind hearing an old man babbling about previous millennia." Josh was enjoying himself now. He lifted his glass, first savoring the bouquet, then sipping the golden liquid with obvious appreciation. "First, I recommend choosing climbs—whatever they may be—that you can do fast and with the minimum of equipment. I've already talked about going fast, but part of that is not weighing yourself down too much. Take a smallish pack, that way you won't be able to carry extra items even if you're tempted.

"What type of gear would I need?" asked Al.

"You'll be up against mixed snow, ice, and rock, so obviously you'll need ice axe and crampons together with boots that'll do double duty. By that I mean stiff enough for crampons, but light enough to climb in, no fancy rock climbing shoes. Almost certainly you'll come across some aid sections and likely as not the cracks will be full of ice, so Friends won't be that useful. Take a selection of pitons and learn how to use them before you go."

"It really comes down to this: move fast and travel light. It'll be cheaper that way in any case, and I didn't notice any Cadillacs in camp. The trip should cost you between $1700 and $2,000, depending on how fat you want to make it. It used to be a lot less of course. You fly to Buenos Aires and then again to Rio Gallegos.

"What's there?" asked Al, wanting the full picture.

"Nothing much, there was nothing at all really, when when I first went there, apart from a military barracks. Argentina has some kind of permanent border dispute with Chile. Nowadays, since the park became more popular, a lot of visitors stop there, so it seems as though just about every other building is a hotel. Anyhow, that's where you want to buy your food. You should find a reasonable selection and it'll be much cheaper than farther on. There is a town called Calafate closer to the park, but it's just about the most expensive place in Argentina."

"Is that the way you went?" Al asked.

Josh nodded. "That's right, two years ago."

"No, I mean before, you know."

Josh drifted back, his memory still very clear. "No, it wasn't that easy, not back then," Josh said with a laugh. "I was alone; my partner, an Aussie, had gotten himself deported at the airport. No visa and no excuses. Americans don't need visas, and we didn't even think about it before we left the States. He was disappointed of course. We'd already been traveling for days, first by train to Mexico City, then by plane, and now he had to retrace his steps. I took the bus all the way from Buenos Aires, not having much money. The fare was only 50 bucks including all my gear, which was quite a load. We had big plans and small budgets in those days, you know, before they marked time." He got another laugh.

"The roads weren't paved from Comodoro Rivadavia and as luck would have it our bus broke down. We waited two hours before another bus stopped to help. All the women and children climbed into the second bus which then proceeded to pushed our vehicle the 240 miles to Rio Gallegos, very exciting at 65 mph. Both the drivers seemed about ten years old."

"Sounds like your van, Drake," interrupted Jesse to general laughter, except from Drake, who glowered.

Despite the laughter and general air of relaxation, the group concentrated on every word as the story developed. Josh leaned back, reaching into a pocket to pull out a pack of cigarettes. He extracted one and lit up.

"Holy mackerel!" Jess exclaimed, "You smoke?"

Drake, who'd been silent since his brush with the waitress, saw a chance to ingratiate himself with the older man while putting down one of the kids at the same time.

"It's holy smoke, nerd—mackerels with holes are rare. Whadya think, Jessie? That everybody eats brown rice, works out and goes without sex like you?"

Josh interrupted before general hostilities could break out. "I know it's a terrible habit but I do enjoy it and I don't plan to live forever."

"I thought you already had," blurted out Jesse, who was less in awe than the others. There was an momentary silence as all eyes focused on Josh. After a while his eyes crinkled in amusement as he laughed good naturedly. The others joined in as the tension eased. Drake asked Niles to please go on with the story.

Josh, after drawing luxuriantly on his smoke, began again. "I stayed in Rio Gallegos at a Russian electrician's house, Pedro was his name I recall. He arranged a lift for me with the road construction crew that was improving the road into the Fitzroy area. I suppose that was the beginning of the end in a sense, an end to the really adventurous days. There was no transportation service at all at that time, so the ride was a real godsend to me, although the road crew was making changes I couldn't even contemplate.

"Now you can ride a bus the whole way to the park on pretty decent roads. It used to be commonplace for bridges to get washed away each spring when the streams were swollen from the mountain snow melt."

"If it's so hard to get there, how do you get back out?" put in Jess.

"As I said, nowadays it isn't hard to get there, you can hop on a bus any time you feel like it, almost, and the same coming out. But yes, it was a problem then. We had to wait for the mail van to come through and scrounge a ride with the mailman. It was a slow ride, but we enjoyed it. We were invited in to every estancia we stopped at. This was standard procedure for our driver because he'd always be offered a little something to drink. I never saw him refuse. 'Just good manners,' he told me. Of course, he wasn't simply the mailman to those people, they led pretty isolated lives with very few visitors. So when the mail came it was a special event, a chance to catch up with the news and gossip from the other ranches, more of a social occasion really. Then when we left, they would always press some little gift on him, a goose maybe, or perhaps a whole ham."

"That's the kind of job I could handle," said Jesse.

Drake snorted derisively. "You can barely handle that car of yours, and that's without any drinks inside you. Not that you can drink either." He winked at Josh, man to man, and drained his glass. "What were you saying, Josh, before you were interrupted?"

"Well, I was telling you guys about travel to the park, but Jesse there wanted to leave before we'd even arrived, so I got sidetracked. Anyway, when you do get there you'll have to get a permit, that's something else that's new. We always used to check in informally with the guardia parque, a little old guy called Jose, who only had nine fingers, I remember. He'd got one bitten off in a fight. Now it's all more official, understandably I guess. When we were first there we virtually had the place to ourselves, apart from the climbers, and there weren't too many of us. We saw maybe a handful of tourists during a two- or three-month stay. Oh, occasionally one of the gauchos would ride by, checking on the sheep.

"Sheep?" echoed Al, sounding mystified.

"That's right." Josh took one last luxurious pull on his cigarette before stubbing it out and gazed ruminatively into the distance for a while before picking up the thread of his narrative. "There were hundreds of sheep roaming about, and pumas, mountain lions, preying on them. There were all kinds of wildlife. We even saw torrent ducks nesting one time."

"What's so special about them?" Drake asked.

"Well, they're supposed to be pretty rare. One of the TV networks sent a team down there a few years back to try to film them. They were there for months, spent who knows how many dollars, and came back with nothing. We weren't even looking for ducks, we just saw them by chance on our way over to the Paine. They are kind of neat to watch, though, they paddle against the stream, even when the river's in spate, quite impressive little critters."

"What do they taste like?" questioned Drake, ever practical.

"I don't know," chuckled Josh, "but the sheep are a different matter. They were a useful addition to our supplies. We roasted them over an open fire—delicious. Naturally, when the gaucho came around we always blamed the mountain lions. I don't know whether he believed us or not, but he never gave us any trouble. To give you an idea how things have changed, there were about 10,000 visitors last year, double the previous year's total. As you as can imagine, all those people are going to have quite an impact on the area. No more wild animals, leastwise very few, and no more sheep, unless you count the tourists." He chuckled dryly at his own witticism. "There are other changes. For example, you aren't allowed to burn wood anymore, not above park headquarters anyhow, and there are restrictions on where you can camp."

"Don't you camp up by the climbs?" asked Al

"No way! You camp down in the park. Laguna Torres is the spot for Cerro Torre, either there or the old Maestri camp. If you want to climb on Fitzroy, you'll have to hike over to the Rio Blanco camp. You guys have to realize this is a very serious place were talking about here. One good storm can dump 20 or 30 feet of snow up on the glacier. In any case, no tent could stand up to winds of 100 miles per hour. So what you have to do is set up camp down below where you make yourself as comfortable as possible. You could be spending a long time there, and probably will be. Then you arrange a kind of an advanced base camp. That's where you stash the gear and supplies you'll need for your climb. But make sure that you mark the spot well."

"How do you do that, if there's gonna be 30 feet of snow dumped on it?" asked Drake, the most alert of the trio.

"Good question. There are two methods that I use. If you know which route you're are going for, you stash the gear at the base of the cliff, close to the foot of the climb, then you fix one end of a rope to it and trail the other end up the cliff face where you secure it, fairly high up. Then when you come back after the inevitable storm you can follow the rope down to the gear. It may take you a while to burrow down through the snow after a big storm, but at least you can find it. If you have more than one route in mind, and aren't sure where you'll be starting from, look for a big boulder, a really big one that looks fairly permanent. Don't forget, the glacier is always on the move. Use the same technique as at the cliff face. Just chose your boulder with care—I lost most of my gear underneath one a few years back. It's still up there, I guess.

"It sounds a bit like climbing in the Himalaya, from what I've read," Jesse observed.

"Well, Hans Kammerlander once said that Patagonia was the most difficult and dangerous place he had ever climbed. It's not just that the weather is so extreme, it's that it can change so suddenly. The weather can go from dead calm to dead serious in—oh—20 or 30 minutes. Then you'll have to make a hasty retreat and that's when mistakes happen. Even if you don't make any mistakes, things can still go badly wrong. It's real easy to lose a rappel rope, for example. When you pull it down from the previous station you've got no control over the free end. The wind can blow it anywhere, it's so fierce. If it gets snagged up somewhere to one side of you, which can easily happen, you're in big trouble. I learned this the hard way, so now I always take along an additional seven-millimeter rope. It doesn't weigh too much or take up much room in your pack. You can safely rap on a seven-millimeter, though some people find it a bit scary."

Josh, who had been nursing an empty brandy snifter for some time, began to look around for the bubbly waitress as all this talking had made him thirsty. His thirst was not to be slaked however, for there came a sudden sharp rapping on the window beside them. As they all turned at the sound they saw a small, though formidable-looking woman, strikingly pretty, and a few years younger than Josh. She alternately pointed at her wristwatch and beckoned to Josh, who looked flustered and sheepish by turns.

"Um, ah well, I guess I'm wanted elsewhere guys. It's been nice talking to you." He stood up, his chair scraping noisily on the stone floor, as the youths chorused their goodbyes. They turned to smile at the dark-haired woman as Josh made his way outside. He placed a hand on each of her shoulders and planted a kiss on her upturned face before turning and waving cheerfully to his new friends .

"Look at them," said Drake, as the couple strolled off hand in hand into the gathering dusk. "Like a couple of kids in love."

Fourteen

Cerro Stanhardt
1988

Five days after leaving Los Angeles, we arrived at Fitzroy National Park in the heart of Patagonia—the "Promised Land." The promise here was not milk and honey, but treacherous climbing in violent weather. It had been nine years, almost to the day, since I had climbed over the, last elusive, ice mushroom on Cerro Torre. I anticipated new adventures of the same magnitude.

Abnormally warm weather greeted our arrival at park headquarters. The four of us—Eliza Moran, Greg Smith, Jay Smith and me—were eager to make a mark in the record book kept by the guardia parque (park ranger). The excessive heat at the lower elevations caused sweat to run off my forehead, stinging my eyes as I staggered under the essential loads up to the base camp. The few clouds that prevailed cloaked the upper half of the Torres—if there is one cloud anywhere in the world, it will be over those three amazing towers.

The heat spontaneously generated huge horseflies that could draw blood through your clothes. Fortunately, God be praised, they were easy prey to a quick swat of the hand, although a direct and solid contact with a crunch was essential for success. Jay's torment was so great that he carried a small tree bough to repel the attackers.

After setting up camp at my favorite location, the weather dictated our reality. Restless frustration structured our lives as day followed day. Jay, the weather man, recorded barometric changes, wind direction, cloud formations and so on. Religious reverence was given to this data, fortunately while eating Eliza's fabulous crepes.

Days became weeks. Infrequent breaks in the weather allowed us to carry a load or two, putting us into position for when the weather improved. These occasional forays afforded us the opportunity to meet other climbing personalities in this magical place—the famous and the unknown seeking the test of Patagonia.

A small, close community developed, in which news and epic stories were enjoyably shared in our sporadic conclaves. Underlying themes always concerned the weather and wind—a common element of experience.

Following the basic laws of probability, the weather finally did clear and the four of us struck out for the prime objective, which for me is to go where no one else has gone or to climb in a style no one else has achieved. The Cerro Stanhardt was still the last unclimbed summit of the three Torres. Every new route on the other two,

Cerro Torre and Torre Eiger, had been established using fixed-rope siege tactics and, just possible, the time was ripe to put it all on the line and go for an alpinestyle first ascent.

The approach to the Torres is short—14 km (8 miles)—but arduous. Someone who was a combination of world-class ice skater, gymnast, bongo boarder, runner, skate boarder, skier, climber and mule would have only minor difficulty. An airline attendant by trade, Eliza had aristocratic features as well as ways. Although a veteran of rock climbing in the United States and trekking in Nepal, she had never carried her own 40 pound pack with all the necessary life-support systems in it. and had always been spoiled by having a trail to follow. It was a hideous experience for her, but she survived with only occasional disillusionments. Independent and self assured, she sported a sense of humor worth waiting for, thousands of great stories, always with some hilarious impersonations.

Greg and Jay reached the rock caves before Eliza and me and started excavating the wind-packed snow inside. I called them the Smith brothers although, they were not related. One look at them would leave serious doubts regarding kinship. Greg hails from Kentucky and sports associated speech characteristics and the firm belief that one centimeter is the most functional length for hair—a belief drafted while serving in the military. With a wispy build like a bird, he is perfectly suited for gymnastic rock climbing, at which he excels. Jay is the multi-purpose functional type much like myself, but in a smaller package. His determination and a wide range of abilities and experience made him optimally endowed for this expedition.

We started up the glacier above shortly past dawn after a not-so-restful sleep. We roped up immediately in memory of New Zealander Phil Herron, who died in a crevasse while attempting the first ascent of Torre Eiger. The new snow obscured lurking crevasses while simultaneously making any progress heavy work.

A couple of hours before dark we situated ourselves in a bergschrund, thankful that the tedious, crevasse-riddled glacier was behind us. Jay and I continued climbing in order to give ourselves a morning headstart. Greg volunteered to cut out a cave of sorts where a roof could be fashioned.

Having fixed three-and-a-half rope lengths, Jay and I soloed down the remaining 200 feet of 60-degree ice, arriving at the bergschrund to discuss the next day's game plan with Greg and Eliza. Feeling a bit spent from her efforts and not wishing to slow the push for the summit; Eliza opted to remain in the security of the bergschrund. Greg, Jay and I decided to make an all out charge for the top and expected to return late that night.

While Jay was cooking the morning meal, part of the overhead snow canopy inconveniently collapsed, half-burying him. At the same moment two other eager climbers arrived, having the advantage of our tracks and fixed ropes up the glacier. Breakfast was postponed and an unwelcome race was on. We passed our guests in the couloir but as the climbing above became more difficult, our threesome couldn't keep pace with the two of them. After eight or nine pitches, their route of choice diverged and the pressure of tense competition eased.

As the weather deteriorated, we continued up the huge ramp system which slashed across the east face and accessed what I had been told would be relatively moderate mixed climbing on the southern wall of Stanhardt. After some unexpected extreme climbing in extreme conditions, we turned tail and commenced a typically epic Patagonian descent in typically epic Patagonian weather. Our tired and tattered trio returned at 1:30 a.m. to an anxious Eliza.

The glacier, moving at an incredible rate, had considerably modified our humble accommodations; the rest of the night was uncomfortable at best. The next day we descended in perfect weather, having no food or fuel. Doing the beer-hall crawl, we awaited the next spell of good weather which we prayed would come before our departure date.

When Eliza, had to return to the States, the three of us decided to raise the ante. We repacked and whittled down the gear, food, fuel and clothing to a minimum and poised ourselves at the starting line, waiting for the barometric starting gun to fire. After two false starts we were off. A steeper, more direct approach, which sometimes stressed realistic unroped climbing, brought us to the col early in the day. Here we unfurled the cords and leashed up. The conditions had changed considerably. What had been easy snow ramps had become poorly protected rock slabs, but familiar terrain allowed greater speed, with Greg in the lead. An early bivvy was established after two hours of chopping out ice platforms. Jay soloed around the corner to have a look at the new choice of route, while Greg and I put the evening's fare on the cooker. Jay returned with chilling stories of what he had seen: "It looks like vertical and overhanging ice, and I want the first four leads," he stated with an air of proclamation. "Judging by your description," I replied, "we won't be coming to blows over it."

He looked at me with a curious wry smile and said, "It will come to blows; it's a funnel and there's no place for you lads to hide. Everything I knock off is going to come right at you."

"We'll make a place to hide," I announced, having already considered that position. "We'll hang the packs horizontally over our heads, one outside the other—that should do the trick."

"OK, we'll find out tomorrow," Jay said.

Doubt is the seed of failure, success the fruit of faith and courage. I hadn't come to Patagonia expecting a promenade; I had been here before and was well aware of what it would take to get the job done. I had conjured the correct images, now was the time for them to take form. A few bumps and bruises weren't going to stop us. Jay and Greg shared the tiny Wild Country tent while I settled into my little scoop on the ice shelf that formed our perch. I tried to calm the tension of excitement within, and get some rest for the night.

We awoke to a special dawn and were off after a quick brew-up. Jay, one of the best ice men in North America, took the business end of the cord as he had demanded. When you want to win, you don't field the second team. The lead was his until he turned it over; there would be no ego games.

Jay dispatched the first pitch, and Greg and I quickly followed. Above us reared a spectacle, a twisted elevator shaft soaring upward. Glistening at the back of the shaft, a narrow wall of glassy ice bulged and curved ever so curiously, precluding a complete view. What we could see would be a test indeed, but that which is hidden is always the most frightening.

The first 60 feet were only about 80 to 85 degrees, but then the face steepened to a real arm-pumping angle. Hanging from one hand, gripping a single ice tool, Jay stabbed a screw into a shallow dimple made with the other axe. It would stick out precariously, threatening to fall out before he could drive it home. No cheater slings for hanging on, to ease this task. "It must be all free," was Jay's war cry. The first all-free ascent on any of the Torres had yet to be done; so we set our sights on this as we looked up the missile silo toward the sky. At the top of this pitch, jammed in a two-foot slot, we bumped and jostled each other as we arranged the packs overhead.

I suggested that Jay pull the camera out of his pack to take a picture looking down, but he was too keyed up to be distracted. Instead he struck out onto the mirrored surface at once, arms burning with lactic fire as he pushed the perimeter of the envelope once more. How much more can he take? I asked myself.

The next pitch was even worse. I could see the grim pain etched on his face, as he pulled from axe to hammer, hammer to axe. Swinging at the concrete surface like an exhausted boxer in the fifteenth round of a championship fight, the pick of the tool struck again and again before securing penetration.

"Ice!" he yelled. A serving-platter-sized piece came crashing towards us. I drove my body against the wall, seeking safety under the packs. Not far enough, I groaned with the brutal impact. My back was bruised and sore from other errant missiles; belaying has its risks.

Struggling for control over distant limbs, Jay fought to place another screw. Stemming wildly behind him, his crampon points scratched for purchase in the thin veneer of ice. The clip-in made, he informed us that this was the most screws he had ever placed on an ice pitch. Three screws later the rope was anchored; he called us up.

When I reached the belay, Jay gestured towards the opposite wall which had been hanging over our heads all the while. From it, a 30 foot column of ice clung precariously by the mere top two feet of its ponderous bulk. Water could be seen running behind it. Hmm, sometimes you get the luck, sometimes you make it. What is fate and what do you create? How often do we cross the line? Or is it just a position in time? Let's keep the Mystery a mystery.

No longer capable of holding the tools, Jay turned over the lead. Greg's silence told me that I was up. Though not the most difficult, the next lead certainly offered the most misery. The surface of the ice was soft and spongy, running with water, while rain fell from toothy icicles that hung in curtains overhead. Into the fanged maw I gingerly ventured.

Why me ? I pondered. Why do I seem to have a penchant for this type of situation? I cursed and pressed onward. In seconds I was soaked to my boots. Protection was poor. The ice was now separated into narrow runnels between rock ribs. I tried placing a screw, but it was no good. I had to go for it; I couldn't stay in this waterfall any longer. Ice was forming on the outside of my clothes, flaking off like breadcrust when I moved.

Mounting a steep bulge, I rushed for shelter under and behind some giant icicles. A 30-foot vertical and overhanging section waited above. I placed a screw and made a dash for it. Coming out around the hanging teeth was awkward and dangerous, but I managed, dislodging only one tooth, which crunched my camera below on the belay.

My forearms were already bulging with blood; I marvelled at Jay's endurance. Stemming against the rock, the final overhang redlined my pumpometer. Like a half-drowned cat, I dragged myself up the final section, anchored the ropes and waited, shivering in the shadows. Jay, then Greg, came up on jumars. Each of them had to be rescued with another rope when their ascenders clogged with ice and refused to hold.

Three more pitches went quickly, as did the day. We raced the sun now, trying to reach the summit before dark. I thrashed with rigging anchors for the descent, while Jay started the last pitch, short but steep. He worked around the summit overhang, and in a few minutes stood on the top. With no anchor available, he used his body to secure the rope. Last up, I pulled over the final wall and ran to congratulate my friends. I extended my hand to Jay, but he passed it by and embraced me with a great hug. The sky was aglow and so were our spirits. Awash with pink in the setting sun the higher summits of the Torre Egger and Cerro Torre, looked so close—but I knew better. Only three shots in the camera with thousand dollar photos everywhere you looked. Who cared? We'd done it. All we had to do was get down. Twenty three and a half hours after leaving the bivouac we returned, three tired but happy lads.

Fifteen

Desmochada
1988

The pinpoint of light flashed like a strobe from wall to glassy wall, then vanished into the blackness of the icy shaft. We had been climbing now for 21 hours straight. If we could just keep it together for a little longer, we'd be safely back to our bivouac site and warm sleeping bags. Greg and I huddled together in obsidian darkness, trying to save his headlamp—mine had already died. I grumbled about the quality decline of lithium batteries. Easter seals or not, this was the last time I would spend $30 for a battery that lasted only twice as long as....I stopped before completing the thought. Something wasn't right. It had been too long since Jay had rappelled down and I hadn't heard his usual cry of "Off rappel." I waited a couple of minutes before going down to see what was wrong, although I sensed that something was. Using the last of our three ropes, I reached his position. The ice was so steep that Jay was struggling to place a screw. His pack pulled him backwards, complicating matters. I pushed him into the ice and he was able to get out of rappel mode.

"I hate rapping in the dark," I muttered. "Be careful," I added as Jay started the next section. "We don't want to blow it now!" We had just made the first ascent of Cerro Stanhardt in the Patagonia Fitzroy area.

We pulled into camp the following day, just after dark. Weary but undaunted, we opened a bottle of wine and celebrated our success. A new tent had sprung up in our camp and soon, prompted by our revelry, the visitor joined our party and conversation in a common tongue. Glen Dunmire was his name and, as it turned out, we, had many mutual friends. Tall and thin, but sturdy, with a friendly unassuming manner, Glen was a river guide who had just been climbing with his father in Peru and had sent his boots home with his dad. Too bad, I thought. Jay and Greg wanted to do the popular southeast ridge of Cerro Torre and at the same time I could be doing the Supercouloir on Fitzroy with Glen. I couldn't let go of the thought; it was too perfect.

A wild thought started to ooze into being. The ooze congealed; Glen and I would go to the town of Calafate for more supplies. Perhaps we would be able to buy some boots from a Norwegian climber who had just left the park, but who would still be in Calafate. After a frantic two days Glen and I were back at the Park with all missions completed, including boots. But there could be no easing of our hurried pace, for the weather had taken an alarming turn for the better and we must run. After 28 non-stop hours from Calafate we arrived at the base of the Supercouloir to find it had changed into the "Super gully," without ice but with abundant falling rocks.

We decided to circumnavigate Fitzroy instead of retracing our ascent route. This would be safer considering the rock-fall danger on our ascent route during the day. With the good weather deteriorating, we started our forced march. We bivouacked that night and the next afternoon arrived back at Park Headquarters. The following morning Jay arrived from camp by helicopter! He and Greg had failed only six pitches from the summit of Cerro Torre, backing off due to overly abusive weather.

Back at camp, a meeting of the High Command was called. Only two summits remained to be climbed in the Fitzroy area since we had climbed Cerro Stanhardt. Of the two, the most appealing was the Desmochada. Jay and I agreed; first ascents were far more important than that fifteenth or sixteenth ascent of the Maestri route on the Torre. Easy for me to say, since I had done it. But Greg wanted to climb the Torre. That was his whole purpose in making the pilgrimage, and, he figured, he had only one more route in him on this trip. Jay, Glen and I would tackle Desmochada and Greg would hope for "two birds in the bush."

With heavy rucksacks, we started on the trail the next morning. But, just as we were heading up the first hill, the noble helicopter arrived. It was to fly a trio of East Germans to the top of Cerro Torre to parapente off for a film. I stopped in mid-stride as light bulbs lit up in my head. I grabbed Glen, who spoke much better Spanish than I, and went down to the helicopter. Sure enough, the

Germans weren't ready and for $40 the chopper would fly us to the head of the glacier, near the base of our climb. What a pleasure it was, better than any limousine. We stepped out after a scenic flight, having saved ourselves three and a half hours of grueling approach.

After picking up some ropes and hardware from our high glacier cache, we began climbing a long ramp system that led up to the base of the wall proper. The ramps, though mostly easy, had one or two tricky spots along with a couple of dicey gullies that had to be crossed. It was in one of these that I glimpsed the sinister scythe-bearer, Mr.D. My tennis shoes were marginal on the hard snow and ice, so I picked my way from rock to rock. I stopped when I heard the terrible whir of falling rocks, and looked up. Safe on the other side, Jay watched with concern as I was caught like a mouse in a rain barrel. The fellow in the black cloak watched, leering. The first rocks went to the right, then a big haymaker came for me. I ducked to the right and it missed by a foot to the left. The guy in black had also left. I crossed quickly and took a break to collect myself after I gained the other side.

Reaching the base of the wall we had a curious surprise when we discovered evidence of a previous bivouac. After dropping our loads we enlarged the bivvy site to make room for three and started down. The next morning we carried the rest of our gear and food up the ramps. Jay and I climbed up to start fixing a couple of pitches, leaving Glen to get water and start a brew. I led up a slanting corner, then stepped onto a polished ramp. It felt tenuous, so I placed a Friend, grabbed it and pulled into a jam. The overhanging rock above leaned but was more secure. A few awkward, strenuous moves later I reached a ledge atop the pillar.

"A bolt—there's a bolt up here!" I yelled down to Jay. "And a rivet below that."

Jay came up. "Wow! what do you think? "he exclaimed, looking at the tell-tale metal protrusions. "I see a sling about a pitch higher, too."

"Maybe they rappelled from there or a little higher" I said. "There was a carabiner on that bolt. They must have left it when they rapped from here."

Jay took the rack and started up. Standing on a European type bolt, his five-foot seven-inch body could barely reach the small holds. He cranked through a couple of moves and stood on some good edges.

"Good moves," he shouted over a slight wind. He surmounted a difficult thin crack and was soon at the belay. I followed and led through. It looked like I could free climb it if not for the degenerating texture of the rock; large flaky scabs coated the interior walls of the crack as it steepened a few degrees. Spontaneously, nasty wounds began appearing on the backs of my hands. I decided that the proven techniques of artificial climbing would be more appropriate.

Reaching the obvious ledge, I quickly inspected for evidence of previous visitors. Nothing. Apparently their high point had been the top of Jay's pitch. We fixed the ropes before descending to the bivvy site where Glen was waiting with coffee. Our faces advertised our feelings of excitement and satisfaction as Glen greeted us. Now if the weather would only hold. In an instant I erased the thought from my mind. I believe one has the power to form at least a part of one's own reality and this shadow which darted through the internal picture was not part of the reality I wished to create.

The morning dawned without gaiety. A grey, diaphanous shroud of high clouds diffused the sunlight. As I looked out from my sleeping bag, I doubted that we would feel the sun's warm rays that day. Dammit, I thought. Everything was going so well—the helicopter ride, the only bolts necessary already in place—I wanted nothing to ruin it. We packed the bags after the perfunctory morning brew and began ascending our fixed ropes. I watched Glen working his way below me, a shadow of doubt darkening his features now and then. He was not with us for his climbing expertise; he was good-natured, easy-going, and happened to be in the right place at the right time.

After a brief pow-wow we decided to see what the weather mode was after two more pitches. We had two more ropes we could fix before we were committed. Jay started the traverse pitch. Dressed totally in red, he punctuated the white and grey world around us. His rock shoes shuffled and padded quietly on the coarse grainy rock. The sound of a piton ringing home broke through the cold rustling of the wind. Tensioning left off the rope he shifted easily to artificial climbing. After some tricky aid placements, and 5.10 face moves, the gap between the crack systems was crossed.

"Well done!" I yelled, in an effort to be heard over the sound of the wind. I followed Jay and fixed a rope across, a bridge for possible retreat that we would leave even if we continued. After relaying instructions over to Glen on how to rig the ropes, I told him to wait there. Jay, anxious to proceed, had already begun investigating the route above when I finished tutoring Glen. While Jay worked his way upward, I kept an uneasy watch over the altimeter. By the time Jay had reached the top of the lead, the belay and I had mysteriously without moving gained 80 feet in elevation (a significant drop in barometric pressure). Another conference and we descended the ropes to wait and see.

Anyone who has retreated in a Patagonia storm will see the logic in this. The altimeter is, of course, a barometer—pressure goes up, altitude goes down and vice-versa—and an 80 foot increase in altitude is something to take notice of. Retreating to the animal comforts of our cosy bivouac site, we waited on the weather. However, the skies didn't change during the rest of the day and neither did the altimeter.

During the night the pressure went up and at first light so did we, bringing all the ropes with us—all except the one across the traverse, which we left as an insurance policy. Jay's lead ended in a little section of aid before a sling belay.

"This is almost like being on El Capitan in Yosemite," I joked. Perhaps in winter, I thought as I chuckled to myself, knowing how quickly it all could change. One minute Easy Street, the next—Skid Row. I passed over Jay, kicking his head to make certain that he was awake, and a little higher knocked a rock on him to be sure that he was alert. He whined and looked up with a scowl, rubbing his head.

"Watch what you're doing, man," he grumbled.

"Sorry about that, but the rock's flaky and these boots don't help."

Free climbing a hand crack, I switched to my Asolo hiking boots. A cry for comfort from my feet had dictated a change from rock shoes. I had acquired a case of trench foot from wet boots on Cerro Stanhardt and my feet were still tender and swollen. To my glee, the pitch ended on some good ledges, allowing a comfortable sitting position. Jay and Glen came up to the ledge and I started the next lead. This pitch was fairly easy—5.9—but fun and intriguing, switching from corner to corner while wondering which to chose and what lay out of sight. The traverse below had led us into the large corner system we were now climbing. Jay charged up a 5.10 hand crack and I led another pitch which started with aid to avoid a crumbly section. Above, a beautiful hand and fist crack brought us to a large ledge; a perfect bivvy spot.

On the next lead, Jay struggled to place some protection in an overhanging, leaning lieback. Finally he managed the crux and yelled down joyously that the climb was now 5.11, A3. I followed quickly and we fixed another pitch of 5.10 before joining Glen on the ledge. The weather still fine and, barring the unforeseen, we would have little problem finishing the climb early and m-a-y-b-e get down to the glacier the next day. Perched high above the curving lines of the glacier, we sat, joking and chatting optimistically.

Dawn broke with yet another great day, and we dashed for the summit. Glen jerked on the haul line as I snapped a few photos while belaying. The climb had become docile and we moved quickly. With only a couple of pitches to go I began hauling the packs, using a sling over a horn as the anchor. There were more pieces to the anchor, but they were out of my sight. I was yarding on the bags when—CRACK! The horn broke and I was away without thought—and in the blink of an eye it was over. I stopped. My hands were bleeding where I had grabbed and hung on the rough rock, the only hold. I don't even remember seeing it. Jay was just turning to see what had caused the commotion. I hadn't even noticed the adrenaline as I hung there, amazed at the indwelling awareness waiting to show its stuff.

An hour later Jay and I were on the summit, the incident forgotten. Below, Glen was in trouble. The rope he jumared had jammed behind a flake of rock, and he was stopped, confounded and becoming terminally distressed. Jay went down to lend a hand and I...I just enjoyed the gusty but beautiful sunny day... I looked down at the glaciers winding and merging, the spectacular Torres thrusting above. Beyond lay the mysterious Hielo Continental. This was better—well, maybe as good as—listening to Bo Diddly. But wait....what's that? The tiniest of cloud puffs, innocently lingering just out west of the Torres—the only cloud in sight. Hmm, it was like an itch that doesn't need scratching...yet.

I was hauling again, after double-checking the anchors, when the bag stuck. Just as the two of them came up I rapped down to free it. The wind seemed to be picking up so I stayed alongside the haulpacks. What about that cloud now? Suddenly that itch needed scratching. Back on top, it was blowing like Chicago in winter, and getting stronger every minute. We had to get down, and fast. Jay was setting the first anchors as I followed Glen, fighting his way in a crouch across the summit slab. Intolerant of his slow passage, I hurried past to help Jay. The wind was ferocious and the cloud had become a monster, consuming us. Instant blizzard; that's Patagonia.

Every rappel is a gamble, every time you throw the ropes you are literally casting your fate to the wind. Luck was with us and we found shelter in a pit formed by a boulder wedged in a gully only three rappels down. To rappel further would be stretching our luck. Tired and thirsty, I thought it would be better to stop where we could get ice to make water as well as a natural shelter. It worked out perfectly and the next day broke beautifully. More rappels, much down-climbing over loose, snow-covered rock led to more rappels and more down-climbing. Finally the glacier—but damn, no helicopter in sight. Happy for the moment, we headed back to camp for another celebration.

Sixteen

Strange Customs
1980

Abroad. Now there's a good, plain, homespun word loaded down with excess emotional baggage—associations, expectations, hopes, dreams, desires. At the sound of those prosaic syllables, even the most earth-bound among us tend to assume a dreamy expression, as who-knows-what beguiling travelogue unravels behind the unfocused eyeballs. Bone-white beaches lapped by sapphire seas, the bustle, noise and color of the bazaar or the souk, exotic food, fabulous wines, the enticements of sensuous dusky maidens, the ancient, dusty pile of the Parthenon, the pellucid depths of a mountain lake and always, the distant shimmer of snowy peaks.

It was the snowy peaks, shimmering or not, that first grabbed my attention and tempted me away from the demi-paradise of California. But whatever the motive, however exotic the destination, however alluring the adventure, however dewy-eyed the traveler, sooner or later reality will intrude. It is an unfortunate fact of modern travel that the first sight one has of any country, no matter how utopian, is the glass and steel-clad enormity of the airport. Furthermore, the first contact with the locals, however winsome they may be, is with the steely-eyed gaze of officialdom.

There are exceptions—some travelers are more equal than others. Certain political panjandrums, visiting dignitaries and so forth, are ushered into the country with nary a glance from the rapacious Revenue Men. They are shepherded through the formalities with obsequious bows from the rabid xenophobe who mans the immigration desk. To a lesser degree, members of the more prestigious mountaineering expeditions (for which I have yet to qualify), are exempt from the worst excesses of the so-called Civil Service. Indeed, I have it on the very best authority (rumor), that the most prominent of British expedition leaders receives the red carpet treatment even before leaving home. While lesser mortals languish glumly in the barren wastes of Heathrow, he is lavishly entertained in the V.I.P. lounge while the plane is readied for him and his entourage.

My own experience at this portal of the 'Sceptred Isle' was less cordial. After several weeks of traveling and climbing in Europe, with the inevitable brushes with bureaucrats, I foolishly anticipated smoother sailing when dealing with fellow English speakers. I could, perhaps, evoke the `Special Relationship' said to exist between our countries. Thus I kidded myself during the short flight from Orly Airport. To say that my reception was a disappointment would be taking British understatement to absurd lengths. My first reaction, when confronted by the snarling churl chosen to welcome visitors to the Kingdom, was that, unknown to me, our two countries had recently declared war. But no, the fellow clearly had an attitude; his belligerence fitted him as well as his immaculate uniform, though admittedly my appearance may have amped his usual level of hostility. My hair, unruly at best, had seen neither scissor nor comb since my departure from the States some months before and was now positively rampant. My clothing, after thousands of miles of meagerly-funded travel might charitably have been described as disheveled. Unfortunately, there seemed to be precious little charity in the offing.

This was a pity because what I needed right then was, if not charity, then at least a little compassion and understanding, although it was doubtful whether these words were found in this geezer's lexicon. My situation was, shall we say, a little delicate. In my haste to make my connection in Paris, I had left my wallet, containing cash, credit cards and passport in the trunk of a car belonging to a French climber who had kindly given me a ride. My benefactor had dashed off with Gallic panache almost as soon as my feet hit the sidewalk—no teary eyed farewells for him. Had I not been carrying my ticket in my pocket, I should have been stranded on French soil instead of the hallowed tarmac of Heathrow Airport. At least here I spoke the language—sort of.

I tried to explain all this to my interrogator, whose face displayed all the warmth and feeling of the concrete pillar by which he stood. Eventually I came to the end of my sorry tale. Or rather, I ran out of steam, reduced to silence by his impassive gaze. I could tell I wasn't getting through. After an eon, I heard him speak although I could swear that not a muscle of his face moved.

"Step this way sir," came the chill, disembodied tones. Suddenly galvanized into action by some unknown stimulus, he abruptly wheeled round and marched stiffly toward an anonymous door. Following forlornly in his wake, I found myself in a bleak, grimy, government-agency, kind of room. The furnishings consisted of a plain wooden table and a chair, cunningly designed to administer a sharp prod to the kidneys to whomever sat in it as I soon discovered. The sole item of decoration was a framed portrait of Her Majesty, seated on a horse and looking about as pleased with her lot as I felt with mine. I sat, brooding on my fate. I vaguely remembered reading stories of 'stateless persons' who were shuttled endlessly around the globe, being rejected at every port of call. The thought of spending the rest of my existence in surroundings such as these, surviving on airline food, was not to be borne. In fact, any time spent in this gloomy hole was too long. Leaping to my feet, I pounded on the locked door until it flew open. An airport cop, who looked about eleven years of age except that his eyes were on a level with mine, entered looking mildly miffed. He started to speak but I was in like flint. I demanded loudly and insistently to be allowed to make a phone call.

"Everyone gets to make a phone call don't they?"

"Yes, well, we'll have to see about that. Meanwhile, how about a nice cup of tea?"

I didn't really think tea would cut it, but as nothing else was offered, I took it anyway.

After a lifetime or two, a phone was triumphantly produced; but who to call? My address book, along with the rest of my valuables, was rattling around France in the back of a Citreon Deux Cheveux. I ransacked my brains for the name of the equipment store in London where I was scheduled to present a slide show, one of a series arranged for my visit. After much coaxing, I managed to persuaded a member of British Telecom to disgorge the number, which I anxiously dialed. The hour was already late, but by some good fortune a couple of the lads were sitting around after store hours, chewing the fat and popping a few warm ones. I explained my plight in a few crisp words, and within a couple of hours a savior appeared at the airport to bail me out. After thanking my rescuer, I slickly extracted an advance payment for the slide show.

In retrospect, I guess I can see the Brits' point of view. After all, I was penniless or appeared to be, and they surely don't want the place overrun with indigents who might batten like leeches onto what's left of their welfare system and suck it dry. Sometimes I feel that wherever we go, whatever we do, there is always some chump with a badge whose sole aim in life is to make the lives of others just that bit more difficult and to spread around their own special brand of joylessness.

Running into trouble when entering a foreign country is one part of the travel experience, but I never expected to have any problem leaving home. Wrong again. En route for the Himalayes, we ran foul of one of the men in suits at LAX airport. A minion from the Treasury Department, he ensured that U.S. citizens didn't take too much of their own money out of the country. The fact that dollars have been hemorrhaging steadily toward the Middle East, Japan and all points of the compass for years was, apparently, beside the point. Never mind that the patient is bleeding to death, let's put a Band-Aid on this scratch.

Normally a pecuniary para-medic such as this poses no threat to my peace of mind—oodles of boodle do not figure largely in my life. Don't bother looking for me in First Class. I travel on a shoe string, often badly frayed. My companion, however, was not only Expedition Leader but also Keeper of the Purse. In this role, he was hefting a bundle of the folding stuff such as most climbers couldn't dream of dreaming about. What tipped off the G-Man, I have no idea. Perhaps, like the Ancient Mariner, he stopped one in three. Whatever his method, he nabbed us. There was no small talk about albatrosses, though, our man was all business. Our luckless leader was put through the bureaucratic mill, emerging at the other end, wrung out and mentally mauled. We'd left ourselves plenty of time so at least we made the plane, and the expedition kitty was intact. As usual, the grey men didn't accomplish anything practical. Still, they did manage to get our trip off to a thoroughly bad start and no doubt they were content.

My skirmishes with authority, in all its guises, have spanned many years and countless engagements. More often than not I have emerged the loser, having been heavily outnumbered. Those instances when I felt that I had gotten away with something, however trivial, are all the more precious for their rarity.

During the course of the Trans Borneo expedition in 1983, some members of the team, myself included, collected various artifacts to bring home. These were partly for keepsakes, but more importantly intended for use in various media presentations to promote and publicize the trip. Our flight home unexpectedly terminated in Japan. After the slow shuffle off the plane, the interminable walk to and wait at the immigration desk, the anxious vigil at the baggage carousel, we made our way toward customs. The bulk of the expedition's vast panoply of luggage was taken care of by the organizers, so we had only to deal with our own personal belongings. In addition to my climbing gear and personal equipment, I carried a six-foot blow pipe, reinforced with a twelve-inch spear tip, honed to a fine edge. My armory was completed by a two-foot-long, razor-edged knife called a perong, tucked snugly into its wooden sheath.

Two lines crept toward customs clearance. In the other stood Slade, another expedition member, similarly accoutered. We reached our respective officials at about the same time. My two weighty rucksacks were quickly dispatched. The perong and the spear/blowpipe, which I held stiffly at my side and which, although sealed in a length of plastic pipe, nonetheless made me feel rather like an extra in an old-time biblical epic, received closer scrutiny. A puzzled, suspicious expression suffused the otherwise bland visage of the customs man. He gestured toward the blowpipe.

"What is that?"

"A blowpipe," I said, "From the jungle. Borneo. Just like that one." I waved in Slade's direction. The man glanced briefly across to the other desk, where his colleague was removing the other spear from its tube before nodding me through. As I stepped gratefully through the barrier, I glanced back just in time to see Slade's weaponry being confiscated by the evidently more zealous official. I quickened my pace and sped toward the exit.

Seventeen

The Eiger, Climb for the World
1991

As the train pulled from the station, I waved farewell to Mark Twight. We had attended the ISPO trade show in Munich, Germany, obliged by our different sponsors to present ourselves. I made what turned out to be an unsuccessful attempt to persuade several companies to contribute money on my behalf to "Climb for The World." This promotional event for the United Nations, with its many ups and downs, had been three years in the works. All the efforts had finally borne fruit. Climbers from all continents were to ascend the Eiger by different routes and meet on the summit. A positive symbol of the people from many countries working together for world peace and protection of the planet's ecological balance, it was a noble effort in which I firmly believed. Furthermore, I had a chance at the North Face, a climb I'd hungered for since reading Heinrich Harrer's The White Spider during my youth. Here I was at age 47 with an opportunity to see a dream come true—with any luck

Mark went out of his way to give me a ride to Interlaken so I could catch the train, and along the way he had filled me in on certain particulars about the climb. Although it had been three years since he'd climbed it, the experience was still fresh in his mind.

Ed Drummond, coordinator of "Climb for the World," allowed me to choose a climbing partner from the assemblage of participants from the assorted nations. A glossy brochure picturing all the representatives from the various nations provided the basis for my selection. Had I been younger and prone to make impractical hormonal choices, my pick would have been a beautiful Argentine girl who let all other options out the door. But being a mature and wiser adult, whose wife had warned him to watch his p's and q's, I made prudence my guide.

The train arrived in Grindelwald at 12:15 a.m., right on schedule. Perfunctorily, as this was Switzerland, I ferried my plethora of baggage off the train, leaving it at the station dock without fear of theft. I walked no more than 200 feet before my quest ended. There at an outdoor bar, having a beer, sat Ed Drummond together with Simon, one of the "Climb for the World" film makers. Synchronicity is a beautiful thing. I walked back, grabbed my bags and returned to the bar for a beer and a chat, interested in the "rival" candidates for the North Face. Ed adamantly stressed the dangers of Silvia Fitzpatrick, the Argentine beauty. The general consensus held that she would be a disastrous partner. "She's a powerful rock climber," Ed conceded, "but unsafe."When he had climbed with her in England, she climbed well but couldn't place protection or had totally neglected to do so, and wasn't well versed in the fundamentals of ice climbing or belaying without fixed anchors. No, she wouldn't do. On the other hand, Ed's preference, the Russian Slava, was quite solid although he spoke little English. However, he hadn't shown up or been heard from for a week. What a choice, I thought, a guy you couldn't talk to or a lunatic chick who couldn't or wouldn't put in anchors, let alone protection.

Though a good cause, what the hell had I gotten myself into? After finishing our beers, we headed up the hill above town to the hotel Ed had secured for the night. Wow! A place to stay for the night made this a posh set-up indeed. A few wrong turns in the dark, then we were there. I threw my things on the floor, crawled into the nearest unoccupied bed and was soon sawing logs.

The next day we moved to Kleine Scheidegg. The night before I hadn't recognized the North Face—the ice fields were gone. Silvia arrived but the whereabouts of the Russian were still unknown. Rooms having been provided for us, we settled in for the following weeks. Introductions took place at dinner that night. Silvia was proof of her photo; just my luck she was an apparent nightmare to climb with. Fully alive and animated with a strong, confident personality, she had a charming wild streak not far from the surface.

Because the Russian Slava was still missing in transit, the next day Ed sent Silvia and me to fix ropes down the western flank. Eventually connecting with others coming up from below, these ropes would remain in place to assure a safe retreat in the event of bad weather and to assist the ascent of John Dove, a blind climber from Britain. A helicopter deposited us together with our 2,000 feet of rope on the summit. Silvia's youthful impatience immediately evidenced when the spools of rope demanded careful attention. It was like watching a mirror image of my younger self, so I let it go, knowing the consequences to be paid later. While dragging twisted and tangled coils of rope down the west flank, her good-natured humor persisted undaunted. Despite the rope snarls we completed the task with relative speed.

Two days before a mandatory press conference in Geneva with the Russian still absent, I suggested to Ed that Silvia and I reconnoiter the broken approach ledges to the real climbing. I could check her out as heir apparent to the North Face in case the Russian didn't show. Ed agreed.

A mid-morning start found us at the base of the Nordwand at 11:00 a.m. This was a test, more or less, of what problems might later present themselves. If, in fact, I had to climb with the young Argentine woman, I might have to sort a few things out, like belay anchors perhaps. She straight away wanted the first lead, in which I indulged her. I was instantly, pleasantly surprised. No reckless abandon here; she was cautious, even somewhat conservative. At the top of the lead she placed two belay anchors, a far cry from my suspicions fueled by rumor. I led a pitch, then she stepped into the sharp end. While belaying, I noticed two other candidates for the North Face walking past difficulties via a circuitous but crafty process. We packed the rope in the sack and followed our mentors, one of whom was obviously a guide familiar with the route. We followed as far as I deemed prudent because I had no helmet—it was holding up a corner of a bed which Silvia had broken within five minutes of arriving in her room. You had to love her. The fine weather had been stable for six weeks. Which accounted for the unheard-of dry conditions on the face. The ice fields were the smallest in the history of man, I was told. What this meant in terms of climbing I would discover the next day when Silvia and I were going to climb the face. She was the only show in town. Therefore—forward.

Awaking to the alarm at 5:30, we dressed and went downstairs, our rucksacks packed, ready for the 6:30 a.m. breakfast promised by the hotel staff the night before. However, breakfast wasn't happening until 7:30, typical of Murphy's Law. One hour later, we drank coffee and ate a croissant each, then headed for the North Wall. By 11:30 we were roped up at the Difficult Crack. Of course, Silvia demanded the first lead and I complied without argument. A fixed rope with loops tied in it supplemented the pitch, and I suggested that she clip the loops for protection. She looked appalled but did as I said. I was happy to see that, after briefly grappling with a smooth section of rock, she latched on and climbed the fixed rope. We didn't need to be wasting time with sport-climbing ethics so low on the route. She led her pitches efficiently, crossing the historic Hinterstoisser Traverse as if she had rehearsed it. Moving with reasonable speed, we reached what was normally the First Icefield, but no more. The Ice Hose too was gone. I felt cheated out of the experience—it wasn't like the story book. We wandered over steep, loose slabs and around steep walls where the Second Icefield should have allowed rapid progress. Fixed pitons and old slings told us that we were not the first to pass this way.

Rocks fell in a steady barrage, a horrifying symphony of death from above. I felt relative impunity from small singing stones even though I'd lost teeth to such a missile on the Grandes Jorasses, but the thick, whirling roar of absolute death left me praying for salvation as I cringed under my puny rucksack. Silvia, on the other hand, seemed obnoxiously oblivious to the danger and feared not. Reaching what was left of the Second Icefield, we put on our crampons under the duress of catapulting stonefall. It was Silvia's lead. Exposed on the naked ice, she addressed the nature of the danger as it smashed the frozen arena around her. Moving with nervous speed, she tried to escape time and place. Place an ice screw and just get out of there, I prayed for her. She reached the sanctuary of a wall above and I was already climbing. I had been for 60 feet; I hadn't wanted her to stop in the death zone. The traverse at the upper edge of the Second Icefield should have been obvious but noooo...Small buttresses protruded down onto the ice and a couple of wrong turns slowed us down. Darkness would soon be upon us and I had hoped to reach the Death Bivouac. I thought we would still make it until I saw two other climbers on the Flatiron heading toward my planned destination. We bivouacked two pitches below, an hour after putting on our head torches. Here two people could lie flat and be fairly safe, or so I thought until a stone ricocheted off my boot. We'd have to wear our helmets. Silvia cheerfully cut salami, cheese and bread, but I noticed fewer stars in the sky than should be present.

We spent a fitful though not unbearable night without sleeping bags and awoke to cloudy skies. Having a radio because of "Climb for the World," I used it to ask for a weather update. Deteriorating conditions: thundershowers that afternoon, worsening the next day. Silvia wanted to go on. The difficult descent made me cringe at the idea of retreat, but I knew better. Down, my judgement told me. It was the right choice no matter how much I dreaded the thought. After hours of what seemed like unending rappels and traverses, we encountered the welcoming face of Edwin Drummond who greeted us with hot soup, tea and food. Together we walked back to the hotel.

Meeting the press and the other team members took up the whole next day. During the press conference I had the pleasure of meeting the Russian, who was extremely pleasant and strong but spoke little English. I knew that Ed still wanted me to climb with him and make a political statement about Russia and the U.S.A., but I couldn't have cared less. My decision was made; it would be very awkward and uncertain to deal with the complexities of the classic North Wall with someone I couldn't confer with about necessary decisions. I explained my choice of Silvia as my partner to Ed. She spoke good English and, although I spoke American, she understood me and was a good climber. Ed having agreed, I told Silvia. She looked confused, not knowing her fate was in my hands nor of the politics that had taken place behind her back. I felt a little guilty at having been a part of it, but so it was.

The next day I rode up on the train to Kleine Scheiddeg while Silvia ran. I then nicknamed her "the beautiful animal," which seemed appropriate. It stormed for two days. As others worked on the mountain, setting up tents, stocking food and essentials for the summit parlay, Silvia and I were pardoned prima donnas allowed to focus on our peremptory goal: the Nordwand. After some thought and investigation, I proposed that we avoid the rubble heap of the lower wall by going up the railway tunnel and emerging near the foot of real climbing. Silvia agreed. The rubble was time-consuming in the dark—we'd done it twice and still found it problematic. The next morning started at 4:00 a.m. It was overcast and warm; I didn't like it. I was soaked with sweat as we walked through the tunnel, our footsteps echoing against the walls. Twenty-one years my junior, she set a difficult pace for me to match. No longer inflamed by the burning imperative of youth, it was hard to feel her urgency to reach the window as soon as possible, but I made the effort to keep up. It was good training, she would have said.

A sharp wind whipped through the window as I set it ajar. Looking out through the darkness, I was not pleased; I knew in my bones that it was not the right day. Silvia was still eager to start, I could feel her desire but, after some obstinacy on my part she relented pleasantly. We returned down the tunnel, climbing the side walls to avoid being run over by the regularly scheduled trains. Clouds engulfed the North Face for the remainder of the day, prompting Silvia to acknowledge that my prudence had been justified after all. In such instances I always felt pleased with myself but I'd been fooled more than once before in making intuitive decisions and left feeling like an idiot. We decided to awake early again the next morning.

When I got up to take a look, it was as clear as a bell. Well, I'll be damned. Silvia got up slowly—for her—but soon shifted gears. She thought it better for me to lead the ice this time while she would lead everything lower down. Not exactly a fair trade but I consented—at least she hadn't demanded to lead the rest of the climb as well. We reached the Difficult Crack at 7:00 a.m. and Silvia took off. As we climbed simultaneously, a rope length apart, I would catch sight of her occasionally as she zipped around another corner. I could hear her singing as she went. This was a delightful new experience for me, a singing partner. She finally stopped and belayed just left of where the Ice Hose had been. I had little time to reflect on the big smile on her face before she shot up the next pitch. We belayed the next few pitches up the slabs to the Second Icefield. Silvia showed good judgement in this as rope drag would make this section hazardous for the leader. It was like climbing on a slate roof with loose shingles covered with gravel. We stopped to put on our crampons as the first volley of excitement roared down from above.

"This is a goddamned, dangerous place," I said to Silvia.

She smiled and sweetly added, "It's a big pile of shit. Get going, I don't want to stay here."

I didn't stop to place screws; all I thought about was getting to the protection of the rock band. Silvia had to start climbing before I reached a belay, just as I had when she led this pitch before. I tied the seven-millimeter trail line off for her to use as a hand line. She literally ran up to where I had been. I'd already begun traversing the top of the Second Icefield: impressed by Silvia's ice climbing ability, I didn't worry a bit about climbing when she did.

Stopping to belay at our previous bivouac, I checked my watch: 12:30. We were moving fast enough. I led up toward the Flatiron as the helicopter came in to film us for "Climb for the World." It flew off, then returned as Silvia followed. 1:30 p.m. The passing of another hour found us at the Death Bivouac eating Mars Bars and grabbing a quick drink of water. The Third Icefield could be climbed above and back down without crampons. A short rappel and we started the Ramp. I cheated by running two pitches together, forcing Silvia to simul-climb. She was not happy; I had taken two good pitches. When I promised not to do it again, she forgave me and flashed her infectious smile.

Near the top of the Ramp I stopped short of the Ice Bulge and brought Silvia up next to me. It was an unhealthy belay but there were no options. Rocks zinged down the icefield above, funneling into our cramped position. Suddenly Silvia screamed and grabbed her face. Oh my God, I thought, what's happened? Blood poured from her hands and I could see that a rock had gotten her. The tip of her nose had been shredded, perhaps even broken. I scooped some snow from the wall and had her hold it to the wound. By rights, she should have been crying but only asked me how bad it was. I lied, of course, assuring her it was minor and would not taint her original beauty. I was angry and upset with myself for stopping in such a place, but there were no alternatives.

The next pitch up the ice took us out of this funnel and near the Brittle Ledges. I climbed as quickly as I could and cursed myself every time I shattered the friable ice, sending it rattling down to where Silvia belayed. Without a word she seconded and led through to the ledges. A walk followed but Silvia counted it as a lead and assured me that she had no intention of giving the difficult pitch to the Traverse of the Gods to yours truly. I had to give her credit, she was durable. Her pitch ended at a good bivouac place with scattered snow nearby to melt for water. We'll stay here, I said. At last she agreed with me on something, but not before questioning the possibility of another bivvy site farther on. I shook my head, incredulous at her willingness to continue and as an answer. Later, while drinking hot tea, she still managed to smile with her shredded nose and blood-covered face, and even laugh although it pained her. Quite a woman. For a moment I wished I was 20 years younger.

The night was cold without sleeping bags but the perfect weather held. Silvia started across the traverse in the morning and I followed as far as the White Spider. Armed with two ice tools to Silvia's one, I led the ice up into the ramp of the Exit Cracks, with Silvia's consent. Higher up she encountered some difficult moves around a corner where the rock became covered with ice. I could hear concern in her voice but she couldn't stop to put on crampons. The rope kept moving up. Higher, a fixed rope across a traverse showed me the way and I belayed at the bottom of a square, inset slot. It seemed the obvious route, but caused Silvia, now 50 feet up without protection, much distress. All of the holds were sloping, smooth and all-too-often covered with a nearly invisible veneer of verglas. It had looked so good from below. Looking about, I saw a bolt 15 feet to my left, above a ledge that disappeared around a corner. Hmm, better not say anything, I'd be in big trouble. Besides, it's too late now. Finally she came upon an old fixed pin. Thank goodness, I thought, at least we're not the only people to get lost here. The route apparently rejoined with the square slot variation because my pitch sported several fixed pins. Oh well, Silvia just hadn't been lucky on this climb.

As we continued the Exit Cracks became lower angled. However, normally filled with snow or ice, they were now obnoxious runnels with down-sloping holds filled with loose rubble. Just the rope running over the surface of the loose rocks unleashed dangerous rockfalls. Silvia belayed at the bottom of the final rock slope. We sat and drank water and ate a chocolate bar in the warming rays of the sun. I gave her one of my ice tools and the two ice screws we'd brought; she started toward the summit ridge. A full rope out she placed an ice screw and I started up. Voices greeted our ears from the summit; the "Climb for the World" crew shouted down that they were filming. Two ice screws and three rope lengths later we shook hands with our comrades. On the radio that morning I had ordered a helicopter pick-up off the summit for Silvia—immediate medical attention might save her from being scarred. Charlie Clark, the group doctor on the summit, said it was probably too late for stitches. A scar would preserve Silvia's memory of the Eiger.

Three days later, after climbing the Mittelegi Ridge in one hour and 40 minutes, Silvia danced on table tops at the hotel celebration. You had to love her.

Eighteen

Operation Edison
1972

The plan was a good one. It had been conceived, like many plans, amid the hubbub of the Four Seasons bar, around a table groaning with assorted beverages. Nonetheless the basic idea still seemed reasonable in the calmer atmosphere of the following day. This fact alone was novel enough for us to pursue the matter. The original premise, as I recollect, was more or less as follows.

Camp Four, that sprawling al fresco slum, had been our home for many months, during which time we'd made ourselves as comfortable as our straitened circumstances allowed. Laboriously gathered pine needles created a thick, soft carpet over the site. Awnings over our two tables kept out sun and rain. My large Arabian-style tent was carpeted, hung with printed drapes, equipped with bookshelves and, most important, a box-spring mattress. One way and another, we had created quite a home away from home among the rocks, dust, and pine trees. Now was the time to add the final comfort, the ultimate triumph of technology: Electricity, and with it, Loud Music.

The music was already available, as I owned an old reel-to-reel tape recorder. To obtain the necessary power supply would require more effort, not to speak of ingenuity, resourcefulness, and a fair amount of nerve. I had previously spied a large coil of power cable which lay, apparently abandoned, unused and forlorn in the Park Service maintenance yard. I hate to see anything going to waste, so I decided to find a productive use for this valuable item. After several reconnaissance sorties, we agreed that midnight would be the best time to hit the yard. Experience showed that, at this time, the park security guards would be policing the bars, and no doubt, harassing a few harmless drunks, thus leaving the way clear for us. In the best military manner, George and I synchronized our watches, before making our way, accompanied by 'the boy', to the scene of the operation. After locating the booty, we were just hoisting onto the boy's back, when the dazzling beam of a car headlight pierced the yard. Instinctively, we hit the deck behind a pile of pipes. The boy bravely stifled a groan as the full weight of the coiled copper struck him in the small of his back. Fortunately, we were neither seen nor heard. On our circuitous route home, the boy staggered and stumbled under his load, while George and I attended to the serious business of route finding and scouting for possible danger. Hours later we arrived at the now-slumbering camp.

Now that the first phase of our operation was complete, we attended to the more technical second phase, namely locating and making the necessary connections to a power supply. Delegated to survey the various possibilities, the boy carefully paced out various, crucial distances while appearing to take casual strolls. After evaluating his reports, we calculated that the cable would easily reach from the men's restroom to our campsite. We were set.

We planned to make our move a few nights later, after the moon waned—a hunter's moon. Meanwhile, preparations were underway. While George and I carefully revised the mission over pitchers of beer in the Four Seasons, the lad was dispatched to the store. His mission: to obtain, by any means short of outright purchase, a brown extension lead and a suitable adaptor. The boy returned triumphantly bearing his prize, just in time to buy another pitcher of beer and thus doubly justifying our trust in him. George expertly wired the adaptor and extension to the cable and we were ready for Operation Edison. After some discussion, we agreed to let the boy accompany us for several reasons: first, the cable seemed heavy and, clearly, the lad needed building up; second, the cable had to be routed through a culvert made slimy by recent rainfall and fouled by rotting vegetation: and last, we needed a scapegoat should anything go wrong.

That nothing did go wrong was doubtless due to our careful planning, coupled with faultless execution. As before, we chose our time carefully. In addition, we posted a couple of lookouts. The boy was volunteered to negotiate the oozing mire in the culvert, after first having dug a shallow trench in the intervening ground. George executed the technical task of making the connections and concealing the wire alongside the restroom's brown wooden trim. Meanwhile, I was busy keeping a watch on our lookouts—you can't be too careful. The boy, who was already dirty, was entrusted with the messy, but vital task of burying the remainder of the cable, while we senior officers returned to camp to check on the connections at that end.

For the remainder of that summer, we bathed in the amplified sounds of our favorite bands, and in the enthusiastic approval of our friends and neighbors. We hosted an almost continuous party and were very pleased with ourselves. Not only had we scored a social success, but we had done so at the expense of the hated Park Service. In time, our initial euphoria oozed into bland acceptance; we came to take for granted what had once seemed remarkable. Eventually, the very technology that had brought us so much innocent pleasure brought about our downfall. Planned obsolescence—that was what tripped us up. If we had foreseen it, perhaps we could have forestalled the inevitable. However, we had been living in tents so long that we had forgotten certain basic facts about urban living, in particular, that light bulbs burn out and have to be replaced. Even so, our luck could have been better. As it was, fate sent along a Park Service employee who was not only observant, but curious and persistent too.

His attention drawn by an unexpected flash, this paragon noticed the unusual arrangement of the light fitting. Possessing the aforementioned virtues, he then proceeded to follow our spurious cable to the outside, where it disappeared into the ground. Not content with this, he heaved on the free end, pulling the remainder from concealment, as far as the culvert. With the bit now firmly between his teeth, our hero dove into the half-submerged pipe, emerging at the far end, his temper frayed, his uniform muddied and torn, but with his zeal, unfortunately, undiminished. Observing most of this from his tent, George decided that now might be a good time to examine a boulder problem he had been developing. When he returned much later, he found, to his surprise, the tape recorder still in situ. Missing though, was the cable, which the dutiful employee had, removed. As George gazed at the now defunct machine, an unnatural and oppressive silence reigned over the camp.

Nineteen

Largo's Apprenticeship
1970

I knew them when they were children. Well, children to me. Not that I was old, but I was older and I had been a regular fixture around the Yosemite scene for over ten years. Along with Mark Klemens, Jim Pettigrew and a few others, I had had dominion over bagging new routes, more or less at will, ever since my predecessors had bequeathed the kingdom to me in the late sixties. Of the new generation, a 17-year-old John Long was the first to show up and make known his intention to take the Valley by storm.

One morning Jim Donini strolled over to my camp site located by the generator. He brought news of a recent arrival I had to meet. John Long was his name and climbing was his game. John was brash and outspoken

with a precocious appetite for the most difficult routes—
of which he had a familiar list. Produced by Peter Haan,
this catalog recorded only hard Yosemite routes done in
the past two years. John entertained me with his
contagious enthusiasm as I inspected the list.
Immediately I could see that the record of climbs offered
complications for the Yosemite neophyte: Cream,
Steppin' Out, Basket Case and other climbs on the scroll
were offsized large cracks involving the dreaded
'offwidth' technique, a style of climbing nearly unique to
Yosemite. I understood John was from the greater Los
Angeles area, a Tahquitz regular and doubtless an
excellent face climber.

"Have you done many awful-width cracks?"

"No," he admitted, but blustered on. "But they
can't...and I can....."

"Hmmm, uh-huh," I intoned, suspicious of such
uninitiated pronouncements. These smooth, featureless
fissures were, at best, difficult to protect. Wishing to
humble and not to harm, I offered to usher the lad up an
easy, though exemplary route: the left side of Reed's
Pinnacle. John eagerly agreed and next morning we were
tooling down the road toward Reed's in my '56 Ford. As
we drove, John extolled his abilities, naming the many
test piece face climbs he had mastered. I listened as I
wheeled the old Ford through the series of turns,
knowing that in all probability he would find this route
very different fare.

At the base, John announced his desire to lead the
first pitch, a chimney of confining dimensions. I
thought, Good enough—it would be hard to fall out due
to John's already sturdy stature. Off he charged like bull
at the cape. With a display of power, if not grace, he soon

found himself at the belay. I followed using the practiced technique of a Yosemite regular, and quickly arrived at his side.

With little hesitation I picked through the hardware and selected one nut (knowing the necessary size) and two carabiners, then started off. John looked bewildered, but said nothing, perhaps out of respect. I climbed up, clipped and moved past the bolt—purposely neglecting the rest spot. An interior crack on one side of the main fissure occasionally accepted the chosen nut. But then again, sometimes it didn't. This time it didn't and the nut slid uninhibited and unhindered down to the bolt. John's alarmed voice warned me of the mishap while I moved through the crux section. I replied casually that I was aware of the fallen protection and that it didn't matter. Actually, I had soloed the route several times and felt solid, but certainly didn't want to let on to John and thus ruin the effect of my cool composure.

After dispatching the rest of the pitch, I prepared to belay the lad. He started with robust ease, using his face climbing skills on the large edges that garnished one side of the crack. But the edges vanished at the bolt and the climb became more typical of Yosemite; in a word—smooth. John attacked the crack with force. His muscles bulged and his veins popped. He neared the polished six-inch-wide vertical crux section with little left but courage. Lactic acid crescendoed as panic replaced what little technique he had. He tried to slump onto the rope for a cheater's rest but I was having none of it and paid out slack in kind. If he made it up, I wanted him to know he had done it on his own. His face flushed with effort, his once powerful arms quivered, but his heart wouldn't quit until the synapse collapsed. Just then I took pity and divulged the secret rest hold he hadn't seen behind his back. John's hand shot to it like a chameleon's tongue. Saved! Air flooded into his lungs in great vacuum-cleaner rushes. After a short rest he swam his way to the top and my congratulations.

That evening at camp a friend, Phil Gleason, stopped by and suggested that I have a try at a new route he'd been working on. Fed up with it himself, he offered me the route. As we talked, I could see the keen interest in John's eyes, so suggested that he might come along with Mark Klemens, my usual partner, and me—if he wanted. Without hesitation he grabbed at the chance.

The next morning I was awakened by the drumming of John's pacing feet outside my tent. We threw some gear into a pack and walked to the coffee shop. We were too lazy to make something for ourselves, it was free because the waitress lusted for me as I did for her. After breakfast John still looked confused about the payment of the bill as we rode the shuttle bus toward the climb. The bus took us to the Ahwahnee Hotel, only a short walk from the route. Within a few minutes we stood at the base. As foretold, the flake arched above, leaning and overhanging. We drew stones and Klemens won the lead.

Mark's skills in flaring, overhanging offwidths were beyond reproach and John watched with awe at each precise movement. The flake leaned increasingly until the last eight feet, where it shot out horizontally. A young John Long sat next to me, totally confused as to a solution to this final bit. I'd analyzing the problem since our arrival and had come up with the answer but merely said to John, "You'll see." Klemens showed incredible control while working hard to place protection. John fidgeted nervously. Mark tried again and again to get something in before the crux. A bong would be his preference as he disdained the new fangled nuts, as yet in their evolutionary infancy. He reached to the rack, selected a large I-beam-shaped contraption and announced with typical Klemens' cynicism, "You know I'm desperate now." After using considerable energy fiddling with it, to no avail, he threw it to the ground, cursing. Nearly spent, Mark finally managed to secure a bong, but without the strength to carry on, he lowered to the deck.

My turn. Mark had set it up for me, having done all the hard work of placing the protection. All I had to do was climb and clip. I climbed up to the high point at the crux. John made the mistake of looking away as I slipped quickly through the tricky sequence. I'd gotten two reasonable fist jams, swung down, reached out and pinched the edge of the flake, pulled into a lieback and was resting before the boy from So. Cal. looked up again.

John was outspoken, to say the least but only because he could usually back up his words with action. He started using the pure brute strength of his powerful arms, his feet flailing for purchase. Through the echo chamber of the flake, I could hear his locomotive breathing, amplified. Once again he was desperate, but his great heart and the desire of his ego kept him afloat. He'd thrashed and struggled to the crux, but now hadn't a clue. His life signs ebbed as I shouted down instructions which he followed to the letter. A hand flashed to the finned edge of the flake and his head and torso popped into view, gasping for air. A few power pulls and he'd done it.

"Good job, man!"

John would affectionately become known as Largo to his friends, and he and I would share many great adventures—the Nose in a day, the crossing of Borneo and others—but I'll never forget those first two days.

There were others I met when they first came; Ron Kauk, Werner Braun, Lynn Hill, Maria Cranor and many more. They were children when I first knew them.

Jim "The Bird" Bridwell

For nearly three decades Jim "The Bird" Bridwell has been a leading force in American as well as world climbing. His expertise spans the complete spectrum of climbing disciplines from free climbing on extreme rock to Himalayan peaks. Second ascents of Bridwell routes are often more prized to climbers than a first ascent.

A bold and imaginative style is Bridwell's trade mark and has given him success where others have met with failure. A quest for adventure is not just evident in Jim's climbing.

He has also partaken in some important expeditions for the sake of exploration. Expeditions traversing Borneo, circumnavigating Everest, and exploring the artic ice pack and the wildernesses of western China are some examples. Technical knowledge and expertise has lead to extensive work in the film industry as a consultant and stunt rigging expert. Jim is also a T.V. cameraman and a published writer.

Mountain Biking for Mere Mortals
by Michael Hodgson

Mountain Biking for Mere Mortals
by Michael Hodgson
$6.99 paperback • $8.99 Canada
6x9 inches • 96 pages • 44 cartoons and
drawings • index • glossary
ISBN 0-934802-82-3

A humorous and unorthodox look
at mountain biking
through the eyes of a
mere mortal. Too often,
books on the subject of
mountain biking focus on
the efforts of lycra clad
dare devils on bonsai
missions. Well now the
not-so-gonzo-but-still-
totally-committed enthusiast
will learn techniques for
mountain biking by learning
what is perfectly
unacceptable.

Discover riding techniques to help avoid near
death and other such unpleasantries. Use
etiquette which will not dismay hikers,
equestrians and other bikers. Care for your
steed and master maintenance skills that can
be performed with a mallet. Tour from your
back yard to the wilderness or go where no
sane person would think of going. Prevent

injuries, bumps and bruises. Glue yourself
back together. Explore racing to destroy ego,
body and bike while surrounded by friends.
Also included is a mountain bike
survivalist's dictionary of necessary and
ridiculous terminology.

This book ain't for "team
scream" lycra clad bikers with
huge thighs and lime green
ultra-bright neon duo-tone
bikes with the name "Wild
Thing." It's simply for mere
mortals.

About the author:
Michael Hodgson is an
award winning outdoor
journalist/author and a
member of the Outdoor
Writers Association of
America. In addition to
this book he has written *The Basic Essentials
of Weather Forecasting* and *The Basic
Essentials of Minimizing Impact on the
Wilderness*. He currently resides in San Jose,
CA where he writes an outdoor column for
the San Jose Mercury News and is a
contributing editor for Backpacker
Magazine.

LOOK FOR NEW *MERE MORTALS*
BACKPACKING, IN-LINE SKATING, SKIING
SURVIVAL, CANOEING, RAFTING

ALONG WITH OTHER ICS TITLES AT YOUR FAVORITE OUTDOOR RETAIL STORE.
FOR A CATALOG OR MORE INFORMATION ON A RETAIL STORE NEAR YOU
WRITE OR CALL:
ICS Books, Inc., 107 E. 89th Ave., Merrillville, IN 46410 / 800-541-7323

Climbing Big Walls
by Mike Strassman

CLIMBING BIG WALLS
by Mike Strassman
$8.95 paperback • $11.95 Canada
128 pages • 6x9 inches • illustrations • index
ISBN 0-934802-59-9

Intensive instruction for ascending vertical walls. Big wall climbs are guaranteed adventure. A sport with highly complex gear and extremely demanding techniques, big wall climbing is a rigorous, exciting activity.

Discover your full physical potential while experiencing Nature's splendor. Find harmonies you've never encountered from within yourself. This climbing manual discusses the gear and the support systems required for big wall ascents.

It describes the demanding techniques needed to rise straight up the face of almost any big wall. Climbing ethics and other miscellaneous big wall topics are discussed.

"The climber who is wrapped in a suspended hammock, is looking towards the reader...A larger water bottle is beside him, a sharply cut wall drops straight down for several meters below his eyes and the forest looks like a miniature garden. The striking cover photo of this book captures the thrill of big wall climbing and grabs one's attention.

This is a technical book about big wall climbing featuring first rate personnel like Mike Strassman, Jim Bridwell, Steve Grossman, Randy Leavitt, John Middendorf, and Steve Schnieder.

The contents are divided into 11 chapters, pursuing topics such as general concepts, lead techniques, unloading and cleaning, big wall living, the history of climbing, gear, the use of tricky equipment, speed climbing, solo and first climbs, and ethics."
—THE IWA TO YUKI

"Climbing Big Walls is long overdue and much-needed instructional manual that removes the mystery from one of the most challenging and committing branches of the climbing game ... Although hard-learned lessons are useful because they aren't soon repeated, nobody wants to experiment cold with expando-flake nailing halfway up an A5 nightmare like Scorched Earth. Today, thanks to Climbing Big Walls, nobody has to."
—CLIMBING MAGAZINE

The Basic Essentials of

Mountaineering

by John Moynier

The Basic Essentials of
Mountaineerng
by John Moynier
$5.99 paperback • $7.99 Canada
72 pages • 6x9 inches • illustrations • index
ISBN 0-934802-65-3

Mountaineering can be a dangerous and physically demanding sport. With professional guidance and instruction mountaineering will lead you to peaks of panoramic beauty and of personal achievement. Use this book to supplement professional instruction. Read it BEFORE you begin lessons and you will understand your instruction better.

Correctly use climbing instruments such as the pick axe and crampons. Use good judgment while performing difficult procedures. Develop leadership qualities. Forecast weather changes. Understand the mountain and its environment. Climb snow and ice with greater agility. Gain more respect for mountain hazards.

About the author:
John Moynier is a mountain guide and ski instructor who lives near Mammoth, CA. He has been guiding in his home range of Sierra Nevada for 12 years and is a member of the American Mountain Guides Association. He has climbed throughout the western U.S. and Canada as well as New Zealand and Australia. John is also the author of The Basic Essentials of Cross-Country Skiing.

The Basic Essentials of

Climbing Ice

by John McMullen

The Basic Essentials of
Climbing Ice
by John McMullen
$5.99 • $7.99 Canada
72 pages • 6 x 9 • index • Illus
ISBN 0-934802-87-4

It's not for everyone, but ice
climbing is an essential skill
for mountaineering. Read
this book before you begin
lessons to better
understand your
instructor. Discover a
sport synonymous with
adventure, strength,
e n d u r a n c e ,
perseverance, and
daring.

Read and understand ice conditions.
Implement ice climbing tools such as
crampons, ice axes, and pitons, Use snow,
ice, and rocks as anchors while climbing and

belaying. Ascend, descend and belay vertical
ice faces. Gain the basic yet essential
knowledge to climb vertical and overhanging
ice.

About the Author:

John McMullen is an
author and illustrator
residing in Jackson Hole,
Wyoming. He has worked
on other Basic Essentials
titles as illustrator for The
Basic Essentials of ROCK
CLIMBING, The Basic
Essentials of MOUNTAIN
BIKING, The Basic Essentials
of SNOWBOARDING, the
Beyond the Basics title,
Climbing Big Walls, and most
recently Mountain Biking for
Mere Mortals.

WRITE OR CALL FOR A COMPLETE
LISTING OF THE OVER 30 BASIC
ESSENTIALS TITLES

ALONG WITH OTHER ICS TITLES AT YOUR FAVORITE OUTDOOR RETAIL STORE,
FOR A CATALOG OR MORE INFORMATION ON A RETAIL STORE NEAR YOU:
ICS Books, Inc., 107 E. 89th Ave., Merrillville, IN 46410 / 800-541-7323

The Basic Essentials of

Rock Climbing

by Mike Strassman

The Basic Essentials of
ROCK CLIMBING
by Mike Strassman
$5.99 paperback • $7.99 Canada
72 pages • 6x9 inches • illustrations • index
ISBN 0-934802-45-9

Make it easy to get started in the exciting and demanding sport of rock climbing. Use footholds, hand-holds and toe-locks to nimbly scale verticalfacades of stone. Know the sophisticated technical terms of the sport before you begin lessons, using the glossary for reference.

About the author:
Mike Strassman is a director, author and cinematographer residing in Mammoth, CA. He has worked with some of today's preeminent climbers to produce Moving Over Stone, a video that is recommended to be used with this book.

WRITE OR CALL FOR A COMPLETE LISTING OF THE OVER 30 BASIC ESSENTIALS TITLES

ALONG WITH OTHER ICS TITLES AT YOUR FAVORITE OUTDOOR RETAIL STORE, FOR A CATALOG OR MORE INFORMATION ON A RETAIL STORE NEAR YOU: ICS Books, Inc., 107 E. 89th Ave., Merrillville, IN 46410 / 800-541-7323